THE HEROES AMONG US

Sanjeev Sanyal is an economist and a writer. His bestselling books range from maritime history and economics to satirical short stories. He was born in Kolkata, attended Shri Ram College of Commerce, Delhi, before going to Oxford as a Rhodes Scholar. He currently lives in Delhi, where he serves as an economic adviser to the Prime Minister of India.

Sonia Mehta is a children's author whose books have sold nearly half a million copies and been translated into over eight languages. Her books focus on themes like the environment, value-education, and India. She is the co-founder of Quadrum, a company creating children's books for global publishers. She believes storytelling is the best way to build lifelong readers.

25 Extraordinary Indians

THE HEROES AMONG US

Sanjeev Sanyal
Sonia Mehta

RUPA

Published by
Rupa Publications India Pvt. Ltd 2025
7/16, Ansari Road, Daryaganj
New Delhi 110002

Sales centres:
Bengaluru Chennai
Hyderabad Jaipur Kathmandu
Kolkata Mumbai Prayagraj

Copyright © Sanjeev Sanyal with Sonia Mehta 2025
Illustrations: Mohit Suneja

The views and opinions expressed in this book are the
authors' own and the facts are as reported by them;
these have been verified to the extent possible,
and the publishers are not in any way liable for the same.

All rights reserved.

No part of this publication may be reproduced, transmitted,
or stored in a retrieval system, in any form or by any means,
electronic, mechanical, photocopying, recording or otherwise,
without the prior permission of the publisher.

P-ISBN: 978-93-6156-194-8
E-ISBN: 978-93-6156-873-2

First impression 2025

10 9 8 7 6 5 4 3 2 1

The moral right of the authors has been asserted.

Printed in India

This book is sold subject to the condition that it shall not, by way
of trade or otherwise, be lent, resold, hired out, or otherwise
circulated, without the publisher's prior consent, in any form of
binding or cover other than that in which it is published.

Contents

Introduction / vii

1. Biju Patnaik / 1
2. J.R.D. Tata / 9
3. Sambhu Nath De / 17
4. Salim Ali / 25
5. Indira Gandhi / 33
6. B.B. Lal / 41
7. Verghese Kurien / 49
8. Balbir Singh Dosanjh / 57
9. Major Shaitan Singh / 65
10. Anant Pai / 73
11. Mihir Sen / 83
12. E. Sreedharan / 91

13. Dhirubhai Ambani / 99
14. Nambi Narayanan / 107
15. Rakesh Sharma / 115
16. Kiran Bedi / 123
17. Narendra Modi / 131
18. Bachendri Pal / 141
19. Kapil Dev / 149
20. Krishna Ella / 157
21. Viswanathan Anand / 167
22. Amish Tripathi / 175
23. Yogendra Singh Yadav / 183
24. Mary Kom / 189
25. Neeraj Chopra / 197

Introduction

Every society needs heroes to inspire successive generations to reach greater heights. Which is why their stories need to be retold to every generation. Of course, heroes come in many forms—soldiers, scientists, political leaders, entrepreneurs, sports stars, writers, artists, and so on. Yet, they all share a gritty determination in the face of adversity, the willingness to think out of the box, and the relentless quest for excellence. The authors hope that the twenty-five individuals covered in this book will provide young Indians with an understanding of the range of human endeavours and will inspire them to reach for the stars.

Of course, India has a long and eventful history with many heroes, from Chhatrapati Shivaji to Kalidasa and Aryabhatta. This book, however, limits itself to those who have made their contributions after Independence (indeed this book is being published in the seventy-fifth anniversary year of the Republic of India). Even after having curtailed our scope to this period, we found it difficult to choose just twenty-five individuals. There are a multitude of fields, with countless high achievers in each field. Then there were considerations of diversity by geographical representation, gender, time period, and so on. We additionally had to ensure that the depicted person's achievements were easy to explain to a younger audience. All such choices are ultimately an arbitrary tradeoff made by authors, but we hope it works well for the reader.

The collection includes the multifaceted daredevils Biju Patnaik and Mihir Sen, careful researchers like Salim Ali and Sambhu Nath De, and entrepreneurs like J.R.D. Tata and Krishna Ella. Then there are storytellers like Amish and Anant Pai, brave soldiers like Yogendra Singh Yadav and Shaitan Singh, and the first Indian in space, Rakesh Sharma. Two of India's most consequential Prime Ministers, Indira Gandhi and Narendra Modi, also feature in the collection.

We have made an attempt to tell the story of each individual through vivid anecdotes that illustrate their contributions and their struggles. This is not the place for comprehensive biographies and blow-by-blow accounts. The focus here is to capture a child's imagination. Each section is then accompanied by a

■ INTRODUCTION ■

lively illustration created by Mohit Suneja. Again, they aim to provide some sense of the person's personality to the young reader.

We are grateful to our editor, Yamini Chowdhury, senior development editor Rohan Datta and copy editor Sana Yaseen, for their patient efforts in bringing the book together. We would also like to thank Smita and Dushyant—our respective spouses—for their support.

And finally, we hope that our young readers enjoy this book and are inspired by these heroes to chase their own rainbows.

Sanjeev Sanyal

Sonia Mehta

1

BIJU PATNAIK

Flight of a Daredevil

The young boy ran forward excitedly, his eyes fixed on an object in the sky. It was a small plane making its way towards Cuttack's Killa Fort, where he stood watching it. To his joy, it landed on a nearby airstrip. He rushed over to get a better view, and maybe even touch it.

'STOP!' a guard came in his way. 'You cannot go any further.' The boy turned away, disappointed. He hadn't touched the aeroplane or seen it any closer. But the sight of the landing had lit a fire in the boy's heart. This fire would one day lead him to become a daredevil pilot who performed incredible feats to change the course of India's history.

That boy was Bijoyananda Patnaik, better known as Biju—a pilot, freedom fighter, politician, businessman, industrialist, and philanthropist.

A National Fervour

Biju was born in 1916 in Cuttack in the state of Orissa (now Odisha). It was a time when India was in the throes of British rule. Nationalist sentiment was strong in people as the entire country was coming together to overthrow the British. Both Biju's parents were fiercely committed to India's fight for independence.

Thus, Biju grew up in an atmosphere of great patriotism—something that influenced him enormously. He heard stories of his family fighting against the British and their daring deeds. Already blessed with an adventurous spirit, he also gained a deep sense of justice and human values. Throughout his life, he leapt headlong into adventures, often risking his life to serve a greater cause.

His parents belonged to the middle class. Biju had all he needed for a happy, well-rounded childhood. After finishing school, he enrolled at the prestigious Ravenshaw College.

Once he was done with college, Biju embarked on what was going to become his life's greatest and most enduring adventure. He became a pilot. He joined the Royal Indian Air Force (RIAF) and flew several dangerous missions during World War II, at monumental risk to his own life. This made him a star among British pilots.

The Indonesian Escapade

The year was 1947—an eventful one for India and the world. World War II had ended. India was on the verge of independence. Many other countries were also fighting for independence from their colonial rulers.

Indonesia was one such country. Colonized by the Dutch, the Indonesian rebellion was gaining momentum. Inspired by the Indian freedom struggle, the rebel leaders wanted to consult with people like Jawaharlal Nehru, who was at the helm of India's freedom revolution. By now, Biju had become a close friend and consultant to Pandit Nehru. Knowing of his flying prowess, Nehru reached out to Biju. He wanted to aid Indonesia's cause, for he saw in them a future ally.

In July of that year, President Sukarno asked Sutan

Sjahrir, the former Indonesian Prime Minister, to fly to India for the inaugural Asian Relations Conference. The Dutch, meanwhile, had clamped down hard. Security was tight and no one could leave the country. Airports, railway stations and bus routes were heavily guarded.

'I will fly them out,' declared Biju when Pandit Nehru explained the situation to him. Accompanied by his wife, Gyan, and a small crew of equally adventurous men, Biju's plane entered Indonesian airspace. He landed at a remote, abandoned airstrip near Batavia, now known as Jakarta, the capital of Indonesia.

He ran out of fuel but managed to gather enough leftover fuel from military depots that the Japanese had abandoned. He picked up Sjahrir and other rebel leaders and took off for India. As soon as he was spotted, the Dutch artillery went into action. Guns boomed and bullets flew. Dutch aircraft surrounded him and threatened to shoot him down.

Avoiding gunfire coming at him from all sides, he performed complicated manoeuvres and aerobatics, going higher and higher, until the Dutch aircraft finally gave up. He brought his precious passengers safely to New Delhi.

A Daring Rescue Mission

That was not the end of Biju's daredevilry. The Dutch had started to crack down harder on the rebel leaders in Indonesia. It became critical to get them out of the country before they were killed or arrested. Once more, Biju came to their rescue.

One day, in that same month of July 1947, the Dutch authorities were on high alert. It was two o'clock in the morning and there was a blackout in the country. Stealthily, Biju landed his aircraft on a remote airstrip where the rebel leaders were hiding. Concealed in the shroud of the dark night, he led his small bunch of passengers, including Sukarno and his group of rebels, silently onto his aircraft. Biju would have to take his flight over the sea, crossing more than a thousand extra miles. It was a daring flight, but Biju landed successfully in Singapore, without the Dutch getting even a whiff of what was going on.

Thanks to India's help and Biju's gutsy flights, Indonesia finally gained its independence.

Spy Flights in India

It was now time for Biju to turn to his own country's struggle. On 15 August 1947, India was declared independent. But now, it was divided into two countries—India and Pakistan. The Partition had created immense tensions. There were threats in Kashmir coming across the newly bordered skies. The only way for India to gain the upper hand was to get troops into the Kashmir valley. The Banihal Pass, the only route, was closed. Once again, Biju jumped into the fray. He took a troop of 17 soldiers of the Sikh Regiment and with great dexterity and risk landed on a narrow strip of land in Srinagar. It is said that if not for this mission, the fate of Kashmir might have been different.

Wearing Many Hats

You would think that now that India was independent, Biju Patnaik would leave behind his daring exploits. But the spirit of adventure and the desire to serve his country never left him. By this time, he had entered the political arena and become the Chief Minister of Odisha. Not wanting to lose touch with flying, his first love, he established an airline called Kalinga Airlines.

Biju Babu, as he was now known, never let up on his desire to ensure Odisha's progress. He set up several companies in different industries. He played an important political role in modernizing Odisha, while also working to preserve its culture. Even when he landed in political controversies, he never wavered from his mission to help Odisha develop. During his lifetime, he saw Odisha grow—as a centre of industry, education and culture.

When he died in 1997, Biju Babu left behind a towering legacy as an industrialist, statesman and cultural ambassador. His role as a freedom fighter continues to inspire youngsters.

But above all, his spirit of adventure, his audacious flights, his dangerous missions, and his love of flying are images that endure. He would have loved it so.

2

J.R.D. TATA

The Man Who Gave India Wings

Ten-year-old Jehangir, or Jeh, as his family and friends called him, watched the Zeppelin aircraft flying overhead, during an air raid on Paris. World War I was underway, and Jeh and his family were in their home in Paris. Jehangir was not afraid; he was just fascinated.

'I wish I was older,' Jehangir said to his mother. 'I could have been a fighter pilot and fought the enemy.' He was obsessed with flying and wanted nothing more than to become a pilot and fly his plane. This wistful but childish wish did indeed come true. Jehangir grew up to become one of India's most revered business leaders.

The man who pioneered civil aviation in India went on to steer the destiny of the Tata Group for over half a century, and his love affair with aeroplanes, which began when he was a boy, lasted throughout his life.

A Global Childhood

Jehangir Ratanji Dadabhoy Tata was born in Paris on 29 July 1904. His father was Indian and his mother, French. He was the second of four children. Having spent much of his childhood in France, Jehangir's French was better than his English. His father had deep roots, as well as business interests, in India. Although he loved French life, he frequently took his large family on extended holidays to India.

J.R.D.'s education spanned France, Japan and England. In 1924, when he was just 20 years old, he joined the French army for a year, a mandatory requirement in those days. He wanted to extend his period beyond one year, but his father ordered him to return. J.R.D. hoped to continue his higher education in England.

Fate, however, had a different plan. When he was 22 years old, J.R.D.'s father passed away and he had to take charge of the family business. He renounced his French citizenship and became an Indian citizen.

A Tough Call

Back in India, the Tata family business founded by Jamsetji Tata, J.R.D.'s father's cousin, was growing. With no direct heirs after J.R.D.'s father's death, J.R.D. found himself at the helm of the business. It was a difficult time for young J.R.D. Still in his early 20s, with a largely European upbringing, he suddenly found himself in India, grappling with a new way of life, a new language, and a new work culture, while also figuring out how to manage such a large enterprise. That was not the worst of it. J.R.D.'s father had borrowed heavily, and his debts needed to be paid back.

Taking the bull by the horns, J.R.D. faced his troubles head-on. He sold multiple properties, including their homes in France. All he had left were his shares in the parent company, Tata Sons. Luckily for him, his father had taken him on trips to Jamshedpur, the city that was his great-uncle's vision and the home of Tata Iron and Steel Company (which later became Tata Steel). He was not entirely unfamiliar with the workings of the business. J.R.D. had also seen firsthand the battles his father and uncles fought with the British to keep their business alive. So, there was a nationalistic fervour that burned deep in his heart that was determined to not only save their family business but also grow it.

Following His Dream

As J.R.D. gained a foothold in the business, he turned his attention to his first love, flying.

'I must get a license,' he decided. He became India's first-ever licensed pilot. He learnt how to spin aircraft, perform complicated manoeuvres, and began flying solo. Keeping his family's business and India's needs always in mind, J.R.D. strongly felt that India needed air travel, and that it would be the Tatas who would lead India into the age of aviation. But the time was not right.

J.R.D. decided to do the next best thing. He applied for a license and got it too.

Early one morning in October 1932, an excited J.R.D. climbed into a Puss Moth, the aircraft he would personally fly from Karachi to Bombay with a cargo of mail. He eagerly got into the aircraft as the precious mail was loaded. J.R.D. was triumphant as the aircraft approached Bombay, having flown at the 'dazzling' speed of nearly 100 miles an hour—quite a feat in those days. There were no proper landing strips in Bombay, so he skilfully manoeuvred his aircraft, landing it on the mudflats in the Juhu area of Bombay. There was jubilation on this first flight.

Soon this service became a regular one, undertaken by the airline that was named Tata Airlines. This was a milestone not only in the life of J.R.D. but also in civil aviation in India. For years, this service was used, and despite heavy rains and fierce winds, never once was it disrupted.

An Airline is Born

In 1947, when India finally became independent, J.R.D. decided to spread his wings.

'It's time for India to have her own proper airline that will carry people,' he declared. He approached the government, suggesting that a new airline be set up. Tata would partner with the government to run this airline.

And so, Air India was born.

J.R.D. had big plans for Air India. A stickler for perfection and quality, he ensured that the pilots received the best training. He insisted on the best aircraft. In 1953, the Indian government, under Jawaharlal Nehru, decided to nationalize airlines in India, which meant that the government now had total control over the airline, even though J.R.D. remained chairman—something he was reluctant to do. As the political parties changed, so did the board of Air India.

J.R.D. was asked to step down. Thus ended an era in Indian civil aviation.

From Strength to Strength

Despite Air India no longer under his aegis, J.R.D. was going strong. He had a single goal: to make India self-reliant and create a premium global brand that would be respected the world over. He took the Tata name to different industries. Automobiles, information technology, chemicals, luxury goods, hotels, food, finance—the Tata brand name became ubiquitous in just about every area of life, not just for its business practices, but also for its philanthropy.

J.R.D. began to be recognized across the world for the way he led the Tata empire. Awards and recognitions poured in. The Bharat Ratna, the Padma Vibhushan, and the French Legion of Honour are among the plethora of awards conferred on him for his work. And that is how he will be remembered.

J.R.D. died in Geneva on 29 November 1993 at the age of 89. World leaders attended his funeral. He lived by his principles, always doing what he believed was right.

Ironically, Air India, J.R.D.'s pet project, was bought back by the Tata Group in 2022, 68 years after it was handed over to the government. Had he been alive today, J.R.D. would have been pleased to see Air India back where it belonged.

3

SAMBHU NATH DE

The Quiet Genius

Some heroes are superstars. Some are celebrated and applauded by the world for their achievements. Some work quietly behind the scenes, almost unknown, but do something so important that it changes our lives in the best possible way.

Sambhu Nath De was one such unsung hero. He never won great awards. He wasn't recognized as a great scientist during his lifetime. But his work helped millions of people stay safe from the terrible scourge of cholera—a disease that had been killing people in alarming numbers in India and other countries. And yet, very few people have even heard of this incredible genius.

A Studious Start

Born in 1915 in a village near Calcutta (now Kolkata), Sambhu Nath was a studious young lad. His father was a small business owner who made just about enough money to keep his small family fed. Sambhu Nath was fortunate to have an uncle who showed great interest in the young boy. With his help and a generous contribution from a friendly neighbour, young Sambhu Nath's early education was paid for. He did well at school and was very interested in science and medicine. In 1935, at the age of 20, he was awarded a scholarship to Calcutta Medical College.

It was here that Sambhu Nath met his mentor, Professor M.N. De—the man who would change his life forever. Professor De saw the spark of genius in Sambhu Nath and believed he was meant for bigger things. So impressed was Professor De with the young man that he later even got his daughter married to him. He encouraged him to go to the UCL Medical School in London for his PhD.

'You will get more exposure to what's happening in the scientific community in the rest of the world,' urged Professor De. 'You will also get access to better research facilities.' Sambu Nath needed no further convincing.

In 1939, Dr Sambhu Nath De began his medical practice. But his heart was in research. He didn't just want to cure one person at a time. He dreamt of finding cures that would help millions. That, he was convinced, was how he could significantly contribute to science and medicine and truly make a difference.

The Scourge of Cholera

It was around this time that the fearsome disease of cholera had become a virtual epidemic. Cholera was very infectious and easily passed on from person to person. In the nineteenth century, there were at least three devastating epidemics in Bengal alone, killing thousands. The people of Bengal were frightened, as the dreaded disease seemed to invade every home.

Scientists in different countries had long been working hard to figure out what caused this disease. Louis Pasteur, the French chemist and pharmacist, had spent years trying to get to the root cause. Another scientist, Robert Koch, had theorized what he believed was the key reason why cholera spread so fast and was so deadly. Both scientists examined thousands of patients suffering from the disease. They also studied those who had died from it.

When De came back to India, he was made the Chair of Pathology at the NRS Medical College. At last, he had the resources and the time to focus on his research.

India, at the time, was going through major upheaval. In 1947, it had achieved independence, and the British had left behind a country divided into two parts—India and Pakistan. The Partition had caused a great deal of trauma. Thousands of refugees were pouring into Calcutta. People fell ill with the dreaded Blue Plague—a term given to the cholera epidemic. De made it his life's mission to find the cause of cholera and thereby stop its rampant spread.

Looking beyond

Science is all about making assumptions based on intense research. The assumption that all scientists studying cholera had worked on so far was put forward by Koch. The assumption was that the cholera bacteria attacked the circulatory system and therefore spread through blood vessels in the body.

Scientists tried to study the effect of cholera bacteria on the body by injecting them into the bloodstream of various animals. But the symptoms of cholera simply could not be replicated in the laboratory.

When Dr De studied the hypothesis put forward by Koch, he was not convinced. 'There's something wrong here,' Dr De thought. He felt in his bones that this was not the right direction. He set about doing some intensive research, looking beyond this assumption.

The Breakthrough

'What if the cholera bacteria do not attack the circulatory system but attack the digestive system?' he wondered. He had observed that severe diarrhoea was a symptom of cholera. To explore this thought, he injected cholera bacteria into a part of the intestines of rabbits. Although the rabbits did not suffer from diarrhoea, they died a couple of days later. Dr De felt he was on the right track.

'I must be sure,' he thought to himself. He anaesthetized a rabbit. He then tied a knot on two sides of its intestine, isolating it a few inches from the rest of the digestive system. He next injected the cholera bacteria into this part. He watched and waited.

The next morning, he did an autopsy of the isolated part of the intestine. To his amazement, it was filled with the same whitish fluid that appeared on the stools of cholera sufferers. He had made a breakthrough.

He figured out that cholera spread when people consumed food or water that was contaminated by the cholera bacteria.

Saving Millions of Lives

Now Dr De had a very simple solution to stem the spread of cholera. The key to preventing cholera was to drink clean water, wash fruits and vegetables thoroughly, avoid raw fish and boil water to kill any germs that may have found their way into the food. This was something that even the poorest could easily do. As word of this breakthrough spread, public works authorities across the world also saw the way and improved public sanitation. As people became more aware of these simple solutions, cholera bacteria waned, and millions of lives were saved. This was Dr De's true success.

Not satisfied with this, Dr De continued his research, making several more discoveries and breakthroughs that helped doctors understand the disease and cure patients. So passionate was he about his research work, he would start his experiments every evening, after his hospital duties were done. He also continued to work on Sundays.

Sadly, as he continued his research, he found the

facilities he had access to in India to be inadequate. Feeling stuck and disheartened, he finally retired from the hospital and his research laboratory in 1973. Although he had made such an incredible breakthrough that had saved millions of lives, the scientific community and the world at large did not recognize his work.

In 1978, much after he retired, he was invited to speak at the 43rd Nobel Symposium. '...I feel I have been dead since the early 1960s. I have been exhumed by the Nobel Symposium Committee....' he said in his speech.

It was only after he died in 1985 that many world-renowned scientists acknowledged his contribution to science and medicine. Some of them are known to have said that not recognizing Dr Sambhu Nath De and his groundbreaking work has been one of the world's most regrettable lapses.

It wasn't just his incredible discovery that needs to be acknowledged, but his brilliance and dogged perseverance remain an inspiration to scientists across the world. And most importantly, his breakthrough saved millions of lives across the world from the scourge of cholera.

For someone who started life with meagre resources, this was a feat indeed!

4

SALIM ALI

India's Birdman

Salim Ali rushed home from school. He had to check on the little sparrow he was nursing back to health after it fell out of its nest. The sparrow was obviously feeling better because it was flitting cheerfully around the house, making a nuisance of itself. It wasn't clear to him then—or to those around him—that this fascination with birds would one day make him one of the world's foremost authorities on feathered creatures.

Born in 1896, Ali was the youngest of nine children. Although he lost both his parents when he was little, his uncle Amir adopted the whole brood and raised them in a large house in Bombay (now Mumbai).

In those days, going for *shikaars*—or hunts—was quite the done thing. Uncle Amir had nawabs and rajas in his circle of friends. He was invited to many shikaars and Salim often accompanied him. It was during those expeditions that he became fascinated with wildlife and birds in particular.

The Sparrow Story

One day, when he was about ten, Salim was in Chembur, a suburb of Bombay, which was full of common house sparrows. Salim and his cousins would take potshots at the sparrows with their air guns. He nabbed a sparrow. When it fell to the ground, Salim observed it looked different from the others. It had a yellow stain on its breast as if it had dropped *dal* on it. He showed it to Uncle Amir, who took him to the Bombay Natural History Society (BNHS)—a place that would one day become Salim's home. There, he met a man called Mr Millard, a man after his own heart.

'This isn't a common house sparrow,' Millard said. 'This is a yellow-throated sparrow.' He explained the concept of species and genus. Millard opened up a whole new world for him. At BNHS, round-eyed Salim saw thousands of stuffed birds with details of their species. He was in heaven.

Salim wasn't terribly interested in studying, and he suffered from frequent migraines. When he was 18, his family packed him off to Burma, where his older brother had started a small business. Salim was delighted. He roamed the rubber forests of Burma, observing birds and exchanging information with BNHS, with whom he was now in regular contact.

When he returned to Bombay, he was in better health, and it was time to resume his studies. He studied accountancy in the mornings (urged by his family) and then rushed to St Xavier's College, where he devoured information about animals in zoology classes.

It was around this time that he found his soulmate, Tehmina Begum, a woman from an elite family who had the same love of the outdoors as Salim. Soon after his marriage, Salim was sent to Burma again, this time to help with the family's timber business. As part of his work, Salim had to explore the jungles of Burma to find suitable areas for timber harvesting. These trips were sheer heaven from a birdwatching point of view. Tehmina accompanied him sportingly, joining him in mud-splattered excursions, chasing a bird, sleeping in the huts of Burmese farmers, and camping in forests in the cold.

Back to Bombay

The timber business in Burma didn't thrive and Salim Ali and Tehmina were soon back in Bombay. Ali wanted to find a job that had to do with birds. By this time, he had learnt from Millard how to skin and preserve birds. His knowledge of birds had increased substantially.

Although he didn't get the job he badly wanted—the ornithologist's position with the Zoological Survey of India—because he didn't have a university degree, he managed to get a job as a guide lecturer in the Natural History Department of the Prince of Wales Museum in Mumbai. The profession of an ornithologist, the position he coveted, is the scientific study of birds. Ali came to love his job as a guide. But he soon realized the enormous gaps in his own knowledge.

On a wild impulse, he wrote a letter to Professor Erwin Stresemann, a renowned German ornithologist, asking if he could come there to study under him. To his delight, Prof. Stresemann wrote back, inviting him to Berlin. The next few years were spent in bliss, learning at the feet of a master.

From Prof. Stresemann, whom Ali called his guru, he learnt how to ring birds, that is, attaching labelled tags to the birds' feet to track their movements. He met other greats of ornithology with whom he exchanged ideas, learnt about bird behaviour, taxonomy (the science of classifying birds), and a whole lot more.

When Ali came back to Bombay armed with his new knowledge, he got a rude shock. His old job no longer existed.

On His Own

'I'm done with jobs,' Ali resolved. 'I shall do my own research.' After his sojourn in Germany, his confidence had grown. He decided to study Indian birds on his own. And so began another phase in the life of the adventurous Ali.

India was still under British rule, and many Rajas and Nawabs were happy to support Ali in his research on the birds in their states.

With the loyal Tehmina in tow, Ali spent months doing fieldwork. He was a hard taskmaster. He expected his team to be ready at the crack of dawn to set up tables, clean and polish guns, arrange chemicals to clean the birds, and have notebooks in place to write down their observations. Ali went into deserts, mountains, jungles and rivers to track, capture, classify, ring and observe birds. The team was often without food or water and frequently had to sweat under the merciless sun or trudge through knee-deep mud.

One day, Ali decided he needed to know more about the birds in the Himalayas. He had made several expeditions to the Indian side of the Himalayas. But what about the birds on the other side? He decided to go to Tibet. The valleys were deep with sharp drops.

Ali had spotted a yellow-naped yuhina—a kind of whiskered bird that was rather rare. Ali followed its movements and stood stock-still so as not to disturb it. He was standing on a steep and very narrow trail of loose earth with a drop of hundreds of feet. So engrossed was Ali in observing the bird that he stepped back to get a better view. Suddenly he felt the earth shift below him. A loose pebble slipped from under his foot and went hurtling down into the valley. Ali looked down. To his shock, he was inches away from falling down the side of the valley himself. Heart beating, he steadied himself.

He heaved a sigh of relief as he found himself on firm ground. And then, he went right back to observing the yuhina, who was quite unaware of the interest it was generating.

Ali had many such adventures across the world. Through earthquakes and avalanches, through floods and storms, through scary moments on rickety swinging bridges or in dangerous bandit country—he remained undeterred.

A Global Star

By now, he had gained an international reputation as an expert ornithologist. He authored several books, including the ten-volume *Handbook of the Birds of India and Pakistan*. He also wrote field guides on the birds of different Indian states. He was invited to conferences all over the world. Awards and accolades poured in. Institutions were named after him. A chowk in Mumbai was named Doctor Salim Ali Chowk. And even a species of bat was named *Latidens Salimalii*.

Right up to the day he died at the ripe old age of 90, Ali loved being in nature more than anything. Children adored him and called him Salim *Mamoo*. He spent time with them, teaching them all about birds. Thanks to Salim Ali, now known as the Birdman of India, ornithology, which was once a hobby, became a well-regarded profession.

The sparrow he had rescued when he was a young boy truly changed his life.

5

INDIRA GANDHI

The Iron Lady

Prime Minister Indira Gandhi calmly addressed the nation.

'The war has been forced upon us,' she said in a measured voice.

It was 3 December 1971. Pakistan had launched an attack on India. Tensions had been simmering for a while. East Pakistan, located next to West Bengal, wanted to be a separate country and break away from West Pakistan.

Pakistani President Yahya Khan and commander of Pakistan Army's Eastern Command Lieutenant-General Tikka Khan were furious at this demand. They sent armies to butcher civilians in East Pakistan.

Millions of refugees poured into India to get away from the brutal killings they were subjected to. Mrs Gandhi ensured the refugees were fed, but she knew India could not afford to do this for long.

Mrs Gandhi had been at pains to avoid a military conflict, but she was equally clear that she could not allow such atrocities to happen in India's backyard. She tried to rouse the world's conscience over the savagery and brutal killings of civilians. She visited world leaders in different countries to build support. She met with allies from other countries like Russia and kept them apprised of India's actions.

Acting Decisively

But when Pakistan attacked, Mrs Gandhi took decisive action. She had no intention of being cowed down by anyone. Defiantly, she travelled from outpost to outpost, meeting the troops on the ground, motivating them, and readying them for war. She had alerted her defence chiefs well in advance to be ready for war, and they were. So, when Pakistan launched a series of air strikes against Indian air bases on 3 December, the Indian troops were primed for battle. They fought spectacularly and repulsed the attack.

For 13 days there was furious fighting. The US Seventh

Fleet sailed into the Bay of Bengal, threateningly poised. But the pushback from India was undeterred. On 16 December 1971, 13 days after the first attack, Pakistan surrendered. India was victorious. East Pakistan was liberated and a new country, Bangladesh, was born.

Mrs Gandhi immediately declared a ceasefire. She showed the world that she had no desire to create territorial conflicts. She simply had taken the issue head-on and led it to a successful conclusion, showing her mettle as a plucky, determined leader.

Ironically, this very iron will, and fearlessness, led Mrs Gandhi to take an action that cost her heavily in her later years as prime minister. As a politician, she was a brilliant tactician and strategist but equally ruthless when she didn't get her way. She was fiercely committed to eliminating the debilitating poverty that much of India was struggling with. She made many bold decisions that were milestones during her years as PM. But even as she grew in confidence and power, her way of doing things did not please everyone.

A State of Emergency

She nationalized the banks, which means these were brought under government control. She introduced the

Maintenance of Internal Security Act (MISA), which allowed people to be arrested and imprisoned for a year without giving them a trial. She amended the Constitution at will. In addition, many rebels in India sought to remove her from power. They considered her methods 'undemocratic'. The resistance to her reached such proportions that she took a measure that shook India to its foundations.

On 25 June 1975, she urged then President Fakhruddin Ali Ahmed to sign a document that suspended the Indian Constitution. A state of emergency was declared. This meant that no one had any rights anymore. People could be jailed with no explanation. Media was suppressed. There was state censorship on what people wrote or spoke. This had never happened in the history of India. Anger seethed among the common people.

In 1977, the Emergency was finally lifted, and general elections were held. Mrs Gandhi and her party, the Congress Party, suffered a humiliating defeat. Morarji Desai of the Janata Party came to power as Prime Minister. But this did not last either. There was much infighting within the Janata Party and after the 1980 elections, Indira Gandhi was once again Prime Minister.

A New Problem

Back in the seat of power, she faced a new problem. There was an agitation in Punjab, demanding a separate homeland for the Sikhs—Khalistan. Rebel leader Jarnail Singh Bhindranwale was gaining support. In 1983, in a mob frenzy, Bhindranwale's followers killed six Hindu bus passengers. Riots broke out. Mrs Gandhi imposed President's Rule in Punjab. Bhindranwale's men hid in the Golden Temple in Amritsar, waiting for a moment to hit back. Mrs Gandhi sent the Indian Army to flush out Bhindranwale's men from the Golden Temple. This was Operation Blue Star, during which Bhindranwale and his men were killed. This infuriated his followers, and it was to have a fatal impact on Mrs Gandhi.

On 31 October 1984, just a few months after Operation Blue Star, Mrs Gandhi stepped out of her home in Delhi one morning for an interview. She smiled at Beant Singh, one of her favourite bodyguards. He was a Sikh and had been part of her security detail for years.

To her shock, Beant Singh suddenly opened fire and shot her in the abdomen. Mrs Gandhi died at the All India Institute of Medical Sciences later that afternoon.

A Mixed Legacy

Indira Gandhi's life was fraught with tragedy. She was born on 19 November 1917 in Allahabad. Indu, as she was affectionately known to her grandfather (Motilal Nehru) and father (Jawaharlal Nehru), was a wide-eyed, curly-haired, curious child. Happy though her family was, her childhood was a disturbed one. Many of her family members were important members of the Congress Party and were frequently hauled off to jail for defying the British. Indira came to believe that jail was another home. Her school life was sporadic—sometimes at boarding school, and other times she was tutored at home. As an only child and with the adults around her preoccupied with the freedom fight, she grew to be awkward and lonely.

As she grew up, she naturally became involved in politics. She married Feroze Gandhi, whom she met during her time abroad. Both Feroze and Indira participated in the fight for independence, and even got jailed for a long period. After the death of her father, Jawaharlal Nehru, who was independent India's first Prime Minister, Indira became even more deeply involved in politics. In 1966, she was elected leader of the Congress Party and became India's first female Prime Minister.

Her legacy is filled with great successes and drastic actions. The very strengths she displayed during the war with Pakistan drove her to do things that eventually led to her difficulties. The world remembers her as the 'Iron Lady of India'—a woman who never let anything get in her way.

6

B.B. LAL

The Man Who Brought History Alive

Young Braj Basi Lal looked at the neem tree in the compound of his house with suspicion and fear. Suddenly he shouted. 'Ghost! Ghost! There is a ghost in that tree.' For some reason, he was convinced that the tree was haunted.

His father came running.

'There's no ghost there,' he said, trying to reassure the young boy. But Braj would not be comforted.

'Have you seen the ghost with your own eyes?' his father demanded. When Braj admitted he hadn't, his father advised him to check for himself.

'Take a lantern and climb the tree tonight. Look for it and if you see it for yourself, only then believe that there is a ghost.' Accompanied by a peon from his father's office, a trembling and fearful Braj did just that. Of course, there was no ghost. But the young boy had learnt something that would not just stay with him forever but also remain his guiding light all his life. He would always verify the truth for himself.

This quest for the truth made him one of India's most eminent archaeologists. It is he who shed light on much of India's history, with the discovery of amazing ancient artefacts and architectural remains.

Quite by Chance

Braj Basi Lal, or simply B.B. Lal, as he is better known, was born in 1921 in the village of Baidora, near Jhansi in Uttar Pradesh. It was a complete chance that led him to a career in archaeology. In college, Lal had a burning desire to pursue a master's degree in mathematics. But alas! Math, as it turned out, wasn't meant to be. When it was time to choose his master's subject, he was offered Sanskrit *with* a scholarship, or mathematics *without* a scholarship. Money being tight, he opted for Sanskrit. In his first year, Lal studied ancient epigraphy (the study of ancient inscriptions carved on stone or metal), art, architecture and culture as part of a common course. There was no looking back after that. The bug had bitten him. With his curious and inquiring mind, Lal was smitten by the study of the past.

As a young man, Lal began his career as a trainee under the British archaeologist Mortimer Wheeler. One of his first assignments was to accompany Wheeler on his excavations at Harappa. Lal was a willing, if not always pliant, assistant. He often found himself at odds with Wheeler's conclusions and was never afraid to voice his opinions. Fortunately for him, Wheeler was very open-minded and allowed the youngster to have his say, even if it meant his hypothesis proved wrong sometimes.

The First Breakthrough

The year was 1948 and India was newly independent. The 27-year-old Lal was leading an excavation in Sisupalgarh, near Bhubaneshwar in Odisha. It was here that he made his first breakthrough when he uncovered a site with clear evidence of paved roads, smart housing complexes, and elaborate doorways. He found a fortification wall, eight gateways, and pathways that suggested a township protected by walls. A fort perhaps? Although there were no earlier indications of a fort in this area in any archaeological references, it seemed clear to Lal that this must be the remains of an ancient fort.

Something about the construction patterns rang a bell, and Lal recalled the Sanskrit texts he had studied during his master's. The *Arthashastra*, by Kautilya, was believed to have been written in the 4th century BCE and contained detailed descriptions of what a fort at that time looked like. And those descriptions matched perfectly with what he had uncovered.

'It *has* to be a fort!' exclaimed an excited Lal, dizzy with the possibilities. Most importantly, this discovery challenged the British claim that Indian texts were mere myths and had no place in factual history. Hundreds of years of colonial rule had denied Indians access to their history and culture. Lal was on the verge of breaking this mindset.

A Yawning Gap

Heartened by this discovery, Lal became bolder in his searches. Between the decline of the Harappan civilization in 2000 BCE and the discoveries of 600 BCE, there was a yawning gap of almost a millennium, which he called the 'dark period'. What happened during this period? Who were the people who lived during this time? What was their lifestyle like? Did they build buildings? Who did they pray to? Lal felt an urgent desire to find answers to these questions. He set out looking for answers with his customary zeal.

There were frequent references in the Mahabharata to sites that could possibly answer these questions. Lal began his quest around the Ganga and Yamuna rivers in north-western Uttar Pradesh. What followed was the unearthing of dozens of sites that were clearly linked to events in the Mahabharata through texts or stories—Mathura, Hastinapur, Kurukshetra, Kaushambi, Indraprastha, and many more. During his excavations, Lal also found evidence of game pieces, with the design depicted in the Mahabharata, which were part of the board game *chausar*. It was this very game of chance that made the Pandavas lose to the Kauravas and led to the battle of Kurukshetra.

Ever Curious

Lal's curiosity about the past knew no bounds. He spent hours at various sites, undeterred by rain or heat. The excitement of discovery frequently overrode the need for food or water. Lal and his equally passionate team often found themselves at the mercy of generous villagers who shared what little they had—sometimes sustaining themselves with as little as a fistful of *chana* with jaggery.

By now, Lal's reputation as a skilled archaeologist had grown. He attended excavations and conferences all over the world. He discussed his findings with other archaeologists from other countries. As his reputation and responsibilities grew, he found himself less in the field digging for evidence of the past and more in offices, signing papers, and looking at files. As Director General of the Archaeological Survey of India (ASI), arguably India's most important position in the field of archaeology, Lal was a busy man. But the call and lure of fieldwork and the joy of discovery was too much to resist. He retired from the ASI and joyfully returned to his first love—excavation.

Challenging Beliefs

Lal's curiosity and interest in finding connections between ancient Indian texts and historical findings was as keen as ever. Freed from his administrative responsibilities, he focused on discovering historical links to the Ramayana. It was during these excavations in and around Ayodhya that he first came across what was to become a highly controversial discovery—a Ram temple below a mosque, the Babri Masjid. This finding led to a huge political controversy and many historians dismissed Lal's discovery, calling it nationalistic and communal. Nevertheless, the matter went up to the Supreme Court, where it was declared legitimate. A temple was built on the site where the masjid used to stand.

Lal, no stranger to controversies and naysayers, never backed away from his convictions. He searched for archaeological evidence, and once he had it, his stance was unshakable. As he continued his searches, he came up with yet another theory that contradicted a long-held belief. Based on archaeological evidence along the dry riverbed of the ancient Saraswati river, Lal suggested that contrary to what historians had claimed for decades, the Vedic Aryans were among the original inhabitants of the Indian subcontinent. The issue hasn't been resolved, and even today historians argue vehemently on both sides.

Until the end of his life, B.B. Lal followed the clues his excavations provided to give us all a glimpse into ancient times. The clothes people wore, the coins they used, the kings who ruled—all these are what history is made of. Without this kind of intense effort, we might never have learnt much of India's history. Recognizing his pioneering work, in 2021 Lal was honoured with the Padma Vibhushan, India's second-highest civilian honour.

B.B. Lal died on 10 September 2022 at the age of 101. It seems fitting that a man who brought history alive should live for over a century.

7

VERGHESE KURIEN

The Accidental Milkman

On a Friday, 13 May 1949, a train pulled into a rather ramshackle station in a small milk-producing village called Anand, in the state of Gujarat. A young Verghese Kurien got off the train, full of foreboding. He did not want to be in this godforsaken village—not after experiencing an exciting life in America. 'What on earth will I do here?' he wondered.

Then he gave himself a shake. 'It's only for a short while,' he told himself. He would not have believed if he had known then that this small place would become his life's work, and that he would go on to change India's dairy industry and make milk accessible to everyone in India.

Marching to His Own Beat

Kurien was born on 26 November 1921 in Kerala. His Syrian-Christian family was quite an accomplished one. His father was a surgeon and his mother a pianist. The family placed great emphasis on education. Young Kurien was a good student. He loved physics, and as was the trend in those days, did his engineering. He wanted to join the army, but his mother wouldn't hear of it. So, he ended up joining Tata Iron and Steel Company Limited (TISCO, as the company was then called).

Kurien enjoyed his stint there but wanted to go abroad. He applied for a government scholarship. As luck would have it, he was awarded a scholarship to study dairy engineering. He was taken aback. He had no clue what dairy engineering was and had no interest in it. But he decided to take this opportunity as it would allow him to go overseas.

He made it to Michigan State University in the USA all right, but instead of dairy engineering, he merrily studied his pet subjects—metallurgy and nuclear physics. When he returned to India in 1948, he was in for a rude shock. Not only was this not the India he had left behind, torn apart as it was by Partition, the government was also not at all impressed by the fact that he was now a metallurgical engineer. They wanted a dairy engineer, and that's what they had paid for. They packed him off to a tiny village called Anand, in the milk-producing region of Kaira, to help manage and grow the dairy business.

The Big Challenge

The year was 1949. Kaira was in the throes of a struggle between the dairy farmers and the government. The farmers were fed up with being exploited. Under the leadership of a man called Tribhuvandas Patel, who was himself a freedom fighter, the farmers had been organized into small cooperatives. Each village had its own cooperative. And a union of all these cooperatives was based in the village of Anand. It was to manage this that Kurien was sent to Anand.

Kurien looked around in despair. It seemed to him he had landed in the boondocks. Anand was such a conservative place that no one would agree to rent Kurien a place, all because he was a non-vegetarian. Eventually he found an abandoned, run-down garage where he made his home.

'This is temporary,' he consoled himself as he looked up at the leaky tin roof. He rolled up his sleeves and got down to work. He gave up his glitzy American clothes for a pair of rough overalls, which he began to wear for the difficult job that lay ahead of him. His first task was to tackle the ancient machinery used to produce milk powder in small quantities. With his mechanical bent of mind, Kurien was able to restart them in a jiffy. Now the production of milk powder was increasing, but there wasn't much of a market for it.

Kurien scratched his head. Always a creative thinker, he had an idea. 'Let's approach the biscuit companies,' he decided. 'Surely they need milk for their biscuits, and powdered milk would be perfect for them.' Off he went to Bombay to meet some biscuit manufacturers. Sure enough, he made the sale and set up a milk powder pipeline.

Kurien was buoyed by this early success. But sadly for him, the people around him had got lazy. He felt he was being wasted here. He decided to look for opportunities where he could use his skills better. Before he could find a job, he was convinced by Patel to stay on for a few more months. He agreed, not knowing that he would never ever leave.

Over the next few years, he deep-dived into the dairy business. When he saw the plight of the dairy farmers, how hard they worked, and how little they got in return, he was moved. In his trademark creative style, he did things a bit differently.

Amul is Born

Kaira Dairy registered the name AMUL—a brand that was to enter virtually every Indian household. The name 'Amul' is derived from the Sanskrit word *Amulya*, meaning 'invaluable'. It also stands for Anand Milk Union Limited.

Meanwhile, the dairy farmers in Kaira faced the perennial problem of excess milk during the flush season when the cows and buffaloes produced more milk. The farmers didn't know what to do with all that unused milk and it was getting wasted in huge quantities. Transporting it over long distances to other parts of India posed the danger of the milk spoiling during transport.

Once again, Kurien put his imaginative mind to use. Together with a batchmate, he devised a way to turn the excess milk into condensed milk. Soon Amul's condensed milk was being sold across India. Kaira began to thrive. The experiment of setting up dairy farmer cooperatives was a huge success. But Kaira was still only supplying milk to Bombay and regions in the western parts of India. What about the rest of India?

The White Revolution

India was not producing enough milk to meet the needs of its massive (and ever-growing) population. The Kaira success story made waves—so much so that even the Prime Minister of India, Lal Bahadur Shastri, heard of it. He asked Kurien to do something about India's milk situation. And so began Operation Flood—also called the White Revolution.

Kurien replicated the Kaira model across India. The year was 1970. Kurien travelled across the country, connecting milk sheds and small and large dairy farmers to Mother Dairies in the big cities, where there were many consumers of milk and dairy products. The scheme was so successful that the world noticed. Countries like Russia and Pakistan wanted to replicate this idea and began to set up dairy cooperatives.

Millions of farmers benefited. Milk began to flow and India, a country that had less milk than it required, now had a surplus of it. The mechanical engineer-turned-dairy farmer had triumphed.

Amul's Success Story

In the meantime, Amul had grown from strength to strength. Hundreds of thousands of small milk producers joined hands; many others came on board as managers and technical experts. The Amul brand was making waves, right from the wide range of products, which now included butter, cheese spreads, milk powder, custard powder, cream, and even ice cream, to the adorable Amul Girl, an advertising icon. Sales went through the roof. Kurien built a vast distribution network that helped Amul products reach every corner of India. At every stage, whether it was the colour of the butter, the selling price, or the advertising idea, Kurien applied his own unique brand of creativity and out-of-the-box thinking. Even after his death, Amul continued to grow—becoming the largest milk brand in all of Asia, exporting to several countries.

Kurien left behind an incredible legacy. He helped India go from being a milk-deficient country, where there wasn't enough milk for everyone, to becoming the world's largest milk producer. He helped millions of dairy farmers get their due. When he breathed his last in 2012 at the ripe old age of 91, it was in Anand—the once-ramshackle little village he had put on the world map.

8

BALBIR SINGH DOSANJH

The Man with the Magic Stick

Not all children are crystal clear about what they want to be when they grow up. But this little boy never had a moment's doubt. From the first moment he saw a hockey stick flash at a local game, Balbir Singh knew that was what he wanted to do when he grew up. When he was 12, he watched a newsreel of the Indian team winning a gold medal in hockey at the Berlin Olympics. He was filled with determination to win gold for India one day. He went on to do just that.

The Hockey Dream

Balbir Singh was born on the eve of a new year, on 31 December 1923, in a small village in the Jalandhar district of Punjab. India was in the throes of the struggle for independence against the British. Young Balbir grew up largely without his father, who was a freedom fighter and was frequently jailed.

Not terribly interested in studies, Balbir spent every free moment outdoors, throwing a ball around with a stick. It was clear to anyone who saw him that the boy had talent. He just about made it through school and would never have gone to college if it was not for his hockey prowess. It was his hockey skills that got him admission to the Sikh National College in Lahore (now in Pakistan).

Hockey was the sporting flavour of the times. The Khalsa College and the Sikh National College were spirited rivals. The Khalsa coaches spotted Balbir Singh and poached him to play for them. He led the team to three championship wins. Soon, Balbir was playing for the Punjab team.

The Punjab team had had a 14-year dry patch, not winning anything. Balbir Singh stormed onto the scene and won two consecutive national titles as captain in 1946 and 1947. Now he was truly on the national stage.

Around this time, Balbir Singh got married to Sushil, the love of his life. He had joined the Punjab Police Force so that he could get a salary while playing hockey for his country. With the country in turmoil and Partition riots everywhere, the violence on the streets was getting worse. Balbir Singh took his wife to live in the tiny police quarters next to the Sadar Police Station, where they could be comparatively safe. They lived in a dingy room with no electricity, as India fought its way to freedom.

The Moment of Truth

The year was 1948. It was time for the London Olympics. The Indian hockey team was being picked. India had just gone through a violent and difficult Partition. Punjab, with a top-notch hockey team, was deeply affected as it lay on the border between India and the newly created Pakistan. Balbir saw the horrors of the Partition firsthand—the violence it unleashed and the divisive mindsets it created. Overnight, many of his teammates became citizens of Pakistan, and the Indian hockey team was torn asunder.

Creating a brand-new national hockey team was a challenging task. The Indian selectors now had to put together a team of players, many of whom had never played hockey at this level. Getting them to play as a cohesive team was doubly difficult in the stressful political climate. Balbir Singh was naturally in the selected bunch. The Indian Hockey Federation held many camps and practice sessions to prepare the team for the world's biggest game.

In those days, air travel was a rarity, and the original plan was to send the team to England by ship, which took weeks. However, with the extra sessions, time was running short, so it was decided to fly the team to London. Balbir Singh was in for a rude shock. For no apparent reason, he was dropped from the final team.

Luckily for him, the veteran hockey player Dickie Carr, who had been on the British Indian Olympic team at the 1932 Olympics held in Los Angeles, noticed this. He was shocked that a player of Balbir Singh's calibre was not on the team. He fought for Balbir's place in the team and thankfully for India and Balbir, he got a place on the team.

The hockey league matches started. Balbir Singh was performing at his best. In a league match against Argentina, he scored 6 goals, taking India to a 9-1 victory. To everyone's shock, he was dropped from the quarterfinals and semi-finals against Spain and Holland, respectively. Indian hockey fans were stunned.

A bunch of Indian medical students studying in London at the time were furious. They took up the cudgels on Balbir Singh's behalf. They protested with the Indian High Commissioner, demanding that Balbir Singh be included in the final match. Balbir Singh found a place in the final against England.

Victory at Last

Tensions were running high. As the home team, England had every advantage. The Indian team had made it to the finals, but they had been through a lot of stress on their journey there. The spectators were on England's side. But Balbir Singh was focused. He did not let the tribulations of the last few weeks distract him. In the first half, he scored two brilliant goals, giving India the lead, and the much-needed confidence. With two more goals in the second half, Balbir Singh was clearly the architect of this victory. It was India's first gold medal as a free country.

As he saw the Indian flag being hoisted and the Indian national anthem being played, Balbir Singh's eyes misted over. He had done it! His dream of winning a goal for India had come true. The gold meant the world to the millions of Indians back home. This was the first time independent India's flag had been raised, creating a great surge of national pride and confidence for the entire nation. It was as if they were being recognized by the world.

It was the most important moment in Balbir Singh's life. On their return journey, this time by sea, the team's ship had almost reached the shores of Bombay. But the low tide forced the ship to drop anchor at a little distance from the shore. For two days, the team was stranded on the ship, waiting for the tide to turn. But the fans waiting for them could not wait to see their heroes. A small group of intrepid youth sailed out in smaller boats to greet the winning stars. The hockey team received a rapturous welcome.

Winning Spree

Balbir's hockey dream was not over yet. Four years later, he marched as the flagbearer of the Indian contingent at the 1952 Olympics in Helsinki, Finland. In top form, he scored three goals and led India to victory against England. He followed that up scoring five of India's six goals in a 6-1 win over the Netherlands, to win the gold once again. Of the 13 goals India scored at the 1952 Olympics, 9 were scored by Balbir Singh. He holds the record for the most goals scored in an Olympic hockey final. The

Indian hockey team was now recognized as the best in the world.

Balbir Singh led the Indian team at the 1956 Melbourne Olympics. He scored five goals in the opening match against Afghanistan. India secured the gold medal by defeating Pakistan in the finals.

Balbir Singh Senior (the *senior* was added to his name as there was another Balbir Singh) was a true hockey legend. Called a goal-scoring machine, he dedicated his life to hockey. After his playing days were over, he went on to coach the Indian team, taking it to a World Cup victory in 1975. He was honoured with the Padma Shri, becoming the first sportsperson to receive this coveted award.

Balbir Singh died in Mohali in 2020 at the ripe old age of 96. He was and continues to be regarded as one of the best centre-forwards to have ever played hockey.

9

MAJOR SHAITAN SINGH

A Man, a Hero, a Martyr

Why, you may wonder, does a true braveheart, the hero of a nation and a man who gave his life for his country, have a name like *Shaitan*, which means 'devil' in Hindi? There is a story behind it.

Little Udaibhan went with his father, Major Hem Singh, to the Officer's Mess in Jodhpur. He was a naughty young fellow, as children often are. He was up to some mischief with other children his age when he caught the attention of a British colonel. India was under British rule in those days, and many Indian words were known to the British officers.

'This boy is a real *shaitan!*' the colonel commented. 'You must change his name to Shaitan Singh,' he said to the boy's father. Major Hem Singh was puzzled, for his son, though naughty, wasn't terribly disruptive. But without giving it much thought, he agreed. And Udaibhan Singh became Shaitan Singh, a name that went on to become synonymous with leadership, honour, and bravery in the most dangerous conditions.

The Army Beckons

Shaitan Singh was born into a Rajput family on 1 December 1924 in Jodhpur district of Rajasthan. Shaitan's father was in the Indian Army with the Jodhpur Lancers regiment. Growing up in a military environment, it seemed only natural that Shaitan would also join the army, although he had considered becoming a barrister. But a career in the army won out.

After an arduous course in physical training and warfare at the Officer's Training School in Poona (now Pune), Shaitan Singh became a full-fledged officer of the Indian Army on 3 September 1949. He joined the Kumaon Regiment.

His first posting as an officer was to the freezing climes of Dras in Ladakh. Temperatures there dropped to as low as minus 20 degrees celsius. Along with his unit, Shaitan Singh patrolled the border, which was often under threat by Chinese insurgents. It was the first time he had experienced being so close to enemy lines.

Rising Tension

In those days, there was great tension between India and China. Although historically there had been periods when the two countries tried to be friends and allies, the relationship had deteriorated. *Hindi-Chini Bhai Bhai* was a slogan in the 1950s that hoped to create a spirit of friendship with China. But alas! It did not last. China sought to expand its territories to Indian borders. Tensions between the two countries grew. For India, the main area of worry was that many Chinese maps depicted large parts of Indian regions close to the border as Chinese territory. Clearly, China was trying to edge its way into India, claiming large tracts as its own. India was on high alert.

In October 1962, China attacked India. A fierce land battle followed, with Indian soldiers resisting the onslaught bravely. As the Chinese troops advanced, Indian resistance was strong despite facing heavy mortar and artillery fire from the Chinese. The Indian Army set up nine posts from where their soldiers fired at the approaching enemy. The posts were equipped with small arms and ammunition, sadly less than the enemy had. They struggled with the brutal cold and frozen rations. The Chinese army advanced ruthlessly, mowing down anything or anyone in their way.

Fighting Back Furiously

Indian troops encountered a massive bombardment of mortar and artillery fire. Platoon 7 was attacked by more than 100 Chinese soldiers. Chinese machine guns rained bullets on Platoon 8. The Indian troops were tragically outnumbered. Major Shaitan Singh led the Indian troops as part of Charlie C Company. As the posts fell to the Chinese, the Indian platoons fought bravely, killing several of their enemy soldiers. Many Indian soldiers were martyred during this brutal war.

On 18 November, after over a month of fighting, matters came to a head at a place called Rezang La in the Chusul region of Ladakh. By now, platoons 7 and 8 were virtually wiped out, having come under relentless firing from the Chinese.

Major Shaitan Singh was determined to protect the remaining posts and keep them from falling into Chinese hands. He also wanted to motivate his men and keep them fighting. He moved from post to post, without cover, not caring that he was exposed to a direct bullet. He had already been hit by a bullet in one arm. He decided to go to Platoon 6 to give them some much-needed reinforcement. He had only one thing in his mind: to not allow a single post to fall into Chinese hands. Along with three other soldiers, he dashed towards the Platoon 6 post. Suddenly there was a burst of bullets from the Chinese side. Major Shaitan Singh was hit squarely in the stomach.

Battling on to the End

The brave Major gasped as he fell to the ground. He knew this was the end for him. But he was determined that this should not be the end for India. He ordered his soldiers to leave him and rush to the aid of Platoon 6, which was still holding out. At first, his loyal men refused. They did not want to leave him behind to die. But he was adamant. Reluctantly, they followed the orders of their commanding officer, propping him up with a gun behind a large rock. 'Tell the Commanding Officer and the battalion how well the company fought.' These were his final words to his departing men.

Major Shaitan Singh looked around. He could hear the fighting around him, but he was too badly injured and could barely move. He finally breathed his last, alone, surrounded by freezing snow at an altitude of 16,000 feet. Even though he knew that his troops were fighting a losing battle, he had not given up for a single moment, right up to his dying breath. The battle of Rezang La was the only bright spot in a war that had cost India heavily. Led by Major Shaitan Singh, 120 Indian soldiers had killed nearly 1,300 Chinese men, holding out bravely to the end.

The war ended with a ceasefire on 21 November 1962. China announced its withdrawal from its pre-war position. Major Shaitan Singh's last letter to his family reached them after his death. When they received the letter, they thought he was still alive and even replied. It was only later that they received the tragic news that he had died a martyr.

Three months later, when the snow had melted, the Indian Army and the Red Cross Society launched a search for the fallen soldiers. When Major Shaitan Singh's body was found, he was still holding a gun in his hands.

Major Shaitan Singh was awarded the Param Vir Chakra. Thousands came to his funeral to honour a fallen hero who had fought for his country till his last breath. A memorial was built in Rezang La as well as at his cremation site to salute the martyr. Major Shaitan Singh's village Banasar was renamed

Shaitan Singh Nagar. His statue at the Param Yodha Sthal at the National War Memorial in New Delhi stands witness to a man who may have been named 'devil' but in fact was a 'god' to many.

10

ANANT PAI

The Comic Book Man

On an August morning in 1994, Anant Pai woke up with a start. The phone was ringing. Who could call him so early? Sleepily, he answered the phone. Within seconds, he was wide awake, scrambling to leave the house.

The news he got was the worst possible. A devastating fire had broken out in his office—the place from where he ran his dream projects, *Amar Chitra Katha* and *Tinkle*. Lalita, his wife, watched anxiously as Mr Pai rushed out of the house.

When Mr Pai reached his office, he saw utter devastation. Almost all his stories, artworks and documents had been reduced to charred ashes. He looked around in despair. This had been his dream. He had made it happen. How was he supposed to rebuild it all?

His mind drifted back to those early days, when all he had was just an idea.

The Bombay Years

Mr Pai got to Mumbai (then Bombay) when he was just 12 years old, with his two older sisters. Their parents had died a long time ago, so they had to move in with their grandparents. But even their grandparents passed away, so they ended up moving to Bombay to stay with a relative.

Mr Pai, born in the small village of Karkala on 17 September 1929, missed the place deeply. Karkala was a quaint hamlet in what is now Karnataka. As a child, he often visited the village temple with his grandparents. There, he listened spellbound to the stories told by the priests. At that time, he had no idea telling stories would become his life's work. This early exposure to Indian mythology made Mr Pai very interested in all things Indian.

When he finished college in Bombay, his family forced him to do what everyone did in those days—enrol in an engineering course. Mr Pai hated it. But he had no choice. He became an engineer and got a job. He hated the job. His mind was filled with ideas for writing stories for little children.

One day, Mr Pai, along with his cousins, nieces and nephews, was riding the ferry to Elephanta Caves, off the shores of Bombay. They saw a speedboat zipping past at top speed.

'Wow, look at that boat!' exclaimed his niece. 'It's so beautiful. I'm sure it is foreign-made.'

This got Mr Pai thinking: Why do we instinctively presume that if something is beautiful, it must be foreign-made? Who says we can't create things that are just as good? This thought stayed with him for the rest of his life, and over the years, he tried to change this through his stories.

What's Next?

Mr Pai quit his job. But now he was at a loose end. He didn't quite know what he was going to do, but he knew it would involve storytelling, writing and books. He decided to start a children's magazine called *Manav*. Unfortunately, the magazine didn't do well. Now he urgently needed to find a job. He decided on journalism and joined *The Times of India* in their book division. The publishing bug had bitten him.

Sometimes, luck has a way of helping out. *The Times of India* decided to launch an imprint for children, called *Indrajal Comics*. The comics would feature *Phantom* and *Mandrake the Magician*. But Mr Pai was not happy about bringing only international characters to India.

'What about our Indian characters,' he demanded. 'We have such an amazing culture and history.' He asked the *Times* management to allow him to add sixteen pages of Indian stories. Reluctantly, the management agreed. An overjoyed Mr Pai set about frantically looking for writers and illustrators. In March 1964, after many sleepless nights, the first issue of *Indrajal Comics* was launched—with sixteen pages of Indian stories and sixteen pages of *Phantom*.

The issue was a huge success. Children loved it. It was reprinted many times over.

Mr Pai was overjoyed. But within a couple of years, the management changed their view. The last straw for Mr Pai was when an issue of *Indrajal* once again contained only *Phantom* stories and no Indian stories at all. This was something he could not bear. He now knew that his time at *Indrajal Comics* was coming to an end.

An Idea is Born

One day, Mr Pai and his wife, Lalita, happened to be watching a children's quiz show on television. When the children were asked questions about Greek mythology, they knew all the answers. But when they were asked who Lord Rama's mother was, they hummed and hawed. They came up with answers like, 'Is it Draupadi?' This horrified Mr Pai. He was deeply upset that these Indian children knew more about Western life and culture than their own.

He vowed to change this. But how? Everyone he met felt that no one would be interested in comics with only Indian tales when *Phantom* and *Mandrake* had already captured the imagination of Indian children.

But Mr Pai was convinced that comic books would be the perfect format to tell children all the wonderful Indian tales he had grown up with. He conceived a comic book series filled with only Indian stories. He named his pet project *Amar Chitra Katha*.

Sadly, there were no takers. *The Times of India* turned him down. So did several publishers he approached. Not one to give up easily, he presented his idea to anyone who would listen.

Finally, one day, fortune smiled upon him. A man named G.L. Mirchandani, who owned a distribution house called India Book House, was intrigued by the idea. He agreed to distribute *Amar Chitra Katha*. Mr Pai worked harder than ever. He was a writer, editor, publisher and peon all rolled into one. He plunged into the search for illustrators. He approved of every piece of art himself. Finally, in 1969, the first issue of *Amar Chitra Katha*, *Krishna*, rolled out of the printing press.

It was an instant hit. Within the next ten years, ACK, as it came to be known, was selling a stupendous fifty lakh copies a year, not just in English, but in many Indian languages as well. Millions of children in India and around the world were hooked. They hungrily devoured stories of Puranic heroes, brave kings and queens, and historical figures like Mahatma Gandhi and V.D. Savarkar. Parents watched this phenomenon, both astounded and pleased.

Mr Pai's creative mind was already churning out new ideas. Staying loyal to Mirchandani, who had given him his first break, he launched *Rang Rekha Features*, India's first comic and cartoon syndicate (an organization or agency that sells cartoons to multiple newspapers or publications, helping creators reach a wider audience). *Tinkle*, a collection of fun original stories featuring the goofy Suppandi and the wily Shikari Shambu, was brought out every month.

All this while, Mr Pai along with Lalita never stopped doing what they both loved—meeting children and reading stories to them. At school sessions, through informal gatherings and literary festivals, Mr Pai met thousands of children, telling them stories, and becoming a child with them.

From Mr Pai, he became everyone's beloved Uncle Pai.

Salvaging His Dream

But now, a fire had destroyed everything. Mr Pai gazed at the charred remains of his dream. He still had so many ideas to bring to life, and so many stories to tell.

He called a team meeting to discuss solutions. Every copy of *Tinkle* was burnt along with the positives (photographs of the magazines made before printing). Only some *ACK* positives were stored somewhere and could hopefully be retrieved. Years and years of effort had literally gone up in flames.

Then someone casually suggested, 'Let's get children across India to send us all their old copies of *Amar*

Chitra Katha and *Tinkle*. We can use those to recreate all the comics.'

Mr Pai stared. This was the idea he was looking for. Many thought he was crazy. Like a man possessed, Mr Pai set the ball rolling. He didn't want to miss bringing out the next issue of *Tinkle,* which was due soon. Much of the work had to be recreated. *Tinkle* did not miss its deadline. And an appeal for old issues was made in the magazine.

With *Tinkle* hitting the stands bang on time despite the fire, Mr Pai breathed a sigh of temporary relief. Then he waited. The following week, three enormous packets were delivered. Mr Pai opened them with his heart in his mouth. To his joy, decades-old issues of *Amar Chitra Katha* and *Tinkle* tumbled out. This was just the beginning.

Week after week, children across India joined hands to support their beloved Uncle Pai, and sacks of copies of both publications filled the offices.

It was as if the sun had risen again. Uncle Pai's dream was intact. He had received the greatest gift of all—the deepest loyalty and love from millions of children whose lives he had touched. He went on to create more books, more characters, and tell more stories.

Anant Pai had truly made history. He had opened India to the world of comics. And he had brought Indian tales into every Indian home.

11

MIHIR SEN

The Swimming Sensation Who Never Gave up!

Seven-year-old Mihir looked at his books, trying to study. But his eyes followed his mother, Lilabati, who was bustling about collecting eggs from the hens they kept in their backyard. Lilabati was off to the market to sell the eggs and milk from their old cow to make some extra money.

Little did she know that her boy, living in a dusty village in India, would one day break world records and be bestowed with what are among the country's highest honours—the Padma Shri and the Padma Bhushan.

A Humble Beginning

Mihir Sen was born on 16 November 1930 in a little village in Purulia in West Bengal—17 years before India became independent. His father was a doctor, but what he earned was barely enough to keep the family comfortable.

Mihir's mother worked hard to ensure that he got the best education money could buy. And sure enough, her efforts paid off. One day, when Mihir was eight years old, the family moved to a big city, Cuttack, in the state of Odisha, where the schools were better.

Mihir was a good student and like his mother, an ambitious one. When he finished school and college, he decided to go to England and become a lawyer. He informed his parents of his wish.

His mother, always ambitious for her son, encouraged him wholeheartedly. Going to England was an expensive business, and they did not have enough money. But Sen was not about to give up.

He approached the Chief Minister (CM) of Odisha, Biju Patnaik, for help.

Mr Patnaik didn't take his request seriously. Going to England was quite the flavour of the time, and many young men wanted to go there, often just to enjoy the experience of living abroad. Patnaik had no intention of funding such frivolous pursuits. But he had no idea how deadly serious Sen was.

Sen was not discouraged. For six months, he followed the CM relentlessly. As it happened, Patnaik himself had a great spirit of adventure and couldn't resist a challenge. He saw a spark in the young lad and was impressed by his persistence. He decided to help him. And thus, one day in 1950, Sen packed his bag, boarded a ship, and set off on his adventure to England.

The Adventure Begins

It was tough to survive in a place like England—especially for someone with very little money. But as we've seen, Sen was the kind of young man who never let difficulties get in his way. He found a job at a railway station, working the night shift. Exhausted, he fell asleep on the job one day.

'Wake up, you rascal,' his supervisor prodded him. That was it. He was sacked. Luckily for him, he found work at India House, where Indian students were offered jobs while they studied. He worked all day and studied all night to become a lawyer.

One day, on his way to work, he saw a newspaper on the next seat that someone had left behind. Idly he picked it up. The headline caught his eye. It was about a young woman named Florence May Chadwick, the first woman to swim across the English Channel in both directions.

Sen's eyes lit up. Just the kind of challenge he liked. 'If she could do it, I'm sure so can I!' he said excitedly to himself. But how? He barely knew how to swim. To train, he needed money. He was back to the same old problem.

A Brand-New Challenge

Once again, Sen took matters into his own hands. This time he wrote to the Indian government, and to his amazement, he got a response. He was given a small stipend which he used to begin his training.

He enrolled at the Young Men's Christian Association, and so began Sen's swimming journey. He put in hours and hours and soon mastered the 'free crawl' technique, best suited to conquering the waters of the English Channel. It was time to literally test the waters.

The day was 15 August 1955—India's Independence Day. Sen wanted to gift his feat to his country. Sen looked at the rolling grey sea. He was ready. Taking a deep breath, he leapt into the cold water and began his strokes with powerful strokes. He was just 2.5 kilometres from his goal when a terrible storm struck. Giant waves tossed Sen around like a tiny toy. It was impossible for him to continue. Sen had to abandon his first attempt, even though he was so close to success.

Sen had no intention of giving up. Over the next three years, he tried four times. Each time, there was an obstacle, and he could not complete his mission.

Success at Last

Finally, on 27 September 1958, Sen stood once more, facing the sea. This time, he had chosen the most difficult route on the English Channel. Fifty-three kilometres of freezing water lay ahead of him. He lathered himself with coconut oil, just as he had done in his village. Then he plunged in, swimming with a single thought—getting to the end.

Drawing on his innermost reserves of strength, Sen swam on. The waters were infested with snakes and other creepy crawlies. He kept his eyes and his mind on his goal. Battling rough water, with salt in his eyes, sometimes barely able to see, he swam on. And on. And on.

After 14 hours and 45 minutes, Sen reached his goal

exhausted but triumphant. He stumbled onto the shore, held up a wet Tricolour, and hoarsely sang the national anthem.

He had done it. Sen became the first Asian to swim across the English Channel. He was a hero.

But for a driven and determined young man like Sen, swimming the English Channel was nowhere near enough. He wanted to become the best in the world. He set his sights on other, rarely conquered waters.

He became the first man in the world to swim across the Strait of Gibraltar in around eight hours.

He was also the world's first man to swim across the 40-mile Dardanelles (from Gallipoli in Europe to Seddulbahir in Asia) in just under 14 hours. He swam the Palk Strait between India and Sri Lanka in 25 hours and 36 minutes.

He was the first Indian to swim across the Bosphorus, the river between Asia and Turkey.

He swam the Panama Canal, becoming the first non-American and only the third human in the world to achieve this feat.

His incredible achievements found their way into the *Guinness Book of World Records* as one of the world's greatest long-distance swimmers.

Sen went on to win the ultimate Indian recognition—the Padma Shri and the Padma Bhushan.

He had done it! He had shown the world what true grit and determination were. A long way for a boy from a simple family, born in a remote village in India!

12

E. SREEDHARAN

The Marvels of the Metro Man

The train hurtled past as the young boy watched it, wide-eyed. This was the favourite part of his day. Sreedharan walked four kilometres to school every day with his siblings, and they had to cross the railway tracks. And every day, precisely on time, the train would come thundering along and pass by in an exciting blur. Sreedharan would watch, enthralled by its speed and its sound. This early fascination with trains would become an intrinsic part of his life and earn him the moniker, the Metro Man.

The Lure of Trains

E. Sreedharan was born on 12 June 1932 in the charming village of Karukaputhur in Palakkad district of Kerala. Sreedharan, the youngest of nine children, grew up largely in his mother's ancestral home, as was the custom in those days in that part of India. His eldest sister was 20 years older than him and was like a mother to him. His fondest memory is of his first train journey with his father. The structure of the steam engine, the wooden bogies, the clouds of dust that the engine whirled up—it all seemed like an enchanted world.

When Sreedharan finished college, his fascination for engines and technology drew him to engineering. He got his civil engineering degree and was ready to take up a job. His brother suggested he join the Indian Railways. With his love for trains and engines as alive as ever, Sreedharan thought this was a good idea. However, he had to pass a tough exam, the Indian Railways Services of Engineers exam, conducted by the Union Public Service Commission (UPSC). It was highly competitive, but Sreedharan was nothing if not determined. In 1953, he cleared the exam and began his career with Southern Railways.

As Sreedharan rose through the ranks and gained experience, both technical and managerial, he handled diverse projects. The world noticed him for the way he handled the reconstruction of the Pamban Bridge in Tamil Nadu in record time, after gigantic waves washed it away in a terrible storm.

A Life-Changing Experience

One day, an opportunity presented itself to Sreedharan that would change his life. Calcutta was a city teeming with millions, and transport was an enormous problem. There was a crying need for a mass rapid transport system. The city authorities considered building an underground metro. The advantages were many. It needed the least amount of land, caused minimal pollution, and could carry the most commuters.

Unfortunately, the challenges were also many. Although many countries had had metro rails for years, this would be only the fifth one in Asia and the first in India. As Sreedharan set about making his plans, he realized he and his team had only rudimentary knowledge of planning and building metros. There were issues with deadlines, budgets and approvals. The team had to learn on the job, and finally, the Calcutta Metro trains rolled out. Although Calcutta Metro was India's first, the long delays, multiple engineering issues, and budget overruns only served to highlight to Sreedharan that he still needed to prove that Indians could build world-class metro networks efficiently.

It was clear that Sreedharan's real challenge and triumph was yet to come. He was roped in to mastermind the design, planning and construction of a project that had long been brewing—an ambitious railway corridor that would cross three states—Karnataka, Maharashtra and Goa—and connect hitherto remote towns and villages. Sreedharan was appointed Chairman and Managing Director of Konkan Railway Corporation Limited.

A Formidable Challenge

It was a challenge he could not resist. And a challenge it was indeed. Bisecting the Western Ghats through a terrain of treacherous swamps, rolling rapids, gushing rivers, steep hills and deep forests, taking on environmental concerns, rehabilitating villagers who would be displaced and providing suitable alternatives—these were issues that went far beyond designing blueprints on paper. Sreedharan approached things in his usual out-of-the-box way.

He called on nearly 400 local youngsters, armed with

sturdy mountain bikes, to haul the equipment to places where other vehicles could not reach. He recruited young engineers who shared his passion into his team. Within just eight years from the time the project was kicked off, the first Konkan Railway train was flagged off on 1 May 1998.

The 760-kilometre railway line has 59 stations, 92 tunnels, at least nine of which are more than three kilometres long, 149 large bridges and over 1,800 smaller ones, many going across large waterbodies. The Konkan Railway remains one of the most challenging railway projects and was featured on BBC's Channel 5 series, titled *Chris Tarrant: Extreme Railways*. The Konkan Railway today is a lifeline for millions who live along this corridor.

By now, Sreedharan was at the top of his game, although he had tried to retire once before. But the nation's needs kept calling out to him. This time with yet another project he could not resist—a metro railway for Delhi.

The Metro Marvel

Delhi was reeling under an explosion of commuters. Traffic snarls had become a serious issue. City planners decided that it was time Delhi got a metro.

Naturally, Sreedharan's name was an automatic choice to lead this project. Appointed Managing Director of the Delhi Metro Rail Corporation, Sreedharan took a deep breath and began a new journey.

He was given a budget and a deadline. In all other respects, he was free to do as he wished. With the bitter lessons of the Kolkata Metro strong in mind, Sreedharan started by installing a reverse clock for everyone working on the project to track. The clock was set marking the number of days left until the deadline. Every day at midnight, one day would decrease. This kept the team on their toes, making sure they could plan well in advance.

This small idea was an example of the innovative methods he used to build the Delhi Metro. Challenges popped up all the time, as they do in such large public projects. But Sreedharan tackled them with his usual determination. Built in phases, the complicated project today stands testament to Sreedharan's unique abilities and skills.

Apart from making an engineering and planning marvel, Sreedharan brought his own brand of detail that makes the Delhi Metro stand out. It has features that are unique to India. Sari guards on escalators, a regenerative braking system that saves enormous amounts of energy, and rainwater harvesting on some lines are just some of the ideas that go beyond other metro rail services.

Today, it has a network that stretches 391 kilometres across 12 corridors with 286 stations. It replaces lakhs of vehicles, saving thousands of tonnes of fuel and thereby curbing air pollution.

By now, Sreedharan was known everywhere as the Metro Man. Other cities in India sought his help and followed the Delhi model. In 2008, he was awarded the Padma Vibhushan. The French government awarded him the Knight of the Legion of Honour in recognition of his achievements.

E. Sreedharan's legacy has improved the lives of millions of big city dwellers.

13

DHIRUBHAI AMBANI

No Venture Too Big, No Adventure Too Small!

'Why do you worry so much about money?' a young Dhirubhai impatiently asked his anxious mother, who had to feed her five children on a meagre income. 'I'm going to make lots of money when I grow older, and you will never have to worry about it again,' he assured her. He made good on his promise, years later when he built one of India's most successful companies, placing India firmly on the world map, and establishing one of India's richest business families.

But life didn't begin so rosily for Dhirubhai Ambani. He was born on 28 December 1932 in a small village in Junagadh district of Gujarat. His father was a schoolteacher and barely made enough money to support his large family of five children, his wife, and his parents. The hard life without basic comforts didn't daunt Dhirubhai. In fact, it spurred him on. He was a smart kid, but academic learning didn't interest him at all. He was spirited, with a never-say-die attitude that frequently got him into trouble.

When he had just about finished his school board exams (called matriculation at that time), his father, whose health was failing, told him it was time for him to start helping his older brother earn money to support the family. His brother got him a job in Aden, Yemen. Always ready for an adventure, Dhirubhai immediately agreed and set sail. In those days, Aden was one of the busiest ports in the world, with an enormous number of trading ships passing through.

The Aden Years

Dhirubhai joined a company called A Besse & Co, a firm that dealt with the trading of a vast range of products—from sugar and spices to stationery, tools, machinery, and petroleum products. Dhirubhai was like a sponge, eagerly absorbing all that he could about every aspect of trading.

Dhirubhai lived in a small boarding house with other young Gujarati boys, who were clerks or office workers. During his lunch break, he would wander the bazaars of Aden, meeting traders from different countries hawking their wares. He observed the trade, listened to the gossip in the shipping circles, read every piece of paper he came across, and absorbed every word uttered in the market.

All night, he would read books in English, for he realized that though he was picking up the nuances of trade, he needed to master the English language if he wanted to make it big in the global business world. And that is where he had set his sights.

Slowly, he began trading. At first, he traded in small items, making small profits. He had a sixth sense when it came to reading a deal or indeed reading people. Gradually, he began to borrow money to make bigger deals. Soon he had quite a comfortable nest egg stashed away.

It had been five years in Aden, and Dhirubhai was doing well. He was well-liked as he had a real knack for making friends. He was promoted to the oil-filling station where ships were serviced and refueled. Watching the huge amounts of fuel being poured into the massive ships, he began to dream of one day building an oil refinery. A big dream for someone with such modest roots.

By this time, Dhirubhai had already married a young Gujarati woman, Kokilaben. His time in Aden was coming to an end. He wanted to start his own company. In 1957, he returned to India and founded a yarn-trading company in Bombay. He was just 25 years old.

Back Home

Setting up a home for his young family (he now had a son, Mukesh) in a tiny chawl, Dhirubhai dived headlong into the cut-throat world of yarn trading. He set up a company and called it Reliance Commercial Corporation. His keen eyes observed that a particular type of polyester yarn called *bamber* (or *chamki*, meaning 'shining') was selling like hotcakes. He captured a huge part of this market and received his first big funding for his next venture. This also earned him his nickname, the Polyester Prince.

One day, he decided that just trading yarn was not going to get him the big bucks. He decided to manufacture it.

Boldly, he set up a manufacturing facility in a remote place called Naroda. When the fabric began to roll out of his factories, the established textile manufacturers became nervous. By now, everyone had heard about this brash young businessman who would not let anything stand in his way. The big companies tried to block him by stopping their distributors from buying his fabrics.

Dhirubhai decided to eliminate the distributors. He loaded his small car with his fabrics and went personally from retailer to retailer, selling these at prices far lower than anywhere in the market. No retailer could resist this. Soon, Dhirubhai was the unquestioned king of the textile market and the Vimal brand was born.

'Dhirubhai,' the retailers said to him. 'From now on we will buy ONLY VIMAL.'

Only Vimal. This tagline swept the market and the business world. Named after his eldest nephew, Vimal became synonymous with textiles in India. Reliance was now a serious player in the world of textiles.

Creating Wealth for the Common Man

Dhirubhai believed in making money not just for himself but for everyone. In 1977, he took Reliance

Textile Industries public. He sold shares to the public at just ₹10 per share. His public issue was oversubscribed seven times. Owning a Reliance share was like owning gold. For the first time in India's history, the common man was able to share the success of a business enterprise.

But Dhirubhai was far from satisfied. He decided to move from the production of textiles to the production of polymer fibres from which the textiles were made. From polymers, he went on to manufacture petrochemicals, which were needed to make polymers. From there, he built the oil refineries he needed for the petrochemicals. This strategy of backward integration helped Reliance become a petrochemicals behemoth, adding plastics and power generation along the way.

The Big Bucks

By now, Reliance was one of the largest companies in India with diversified products in different areas. Dhirubhai's two sons, Mukesh and Anil, had taken charge of different areas in the company. His Annual General Meetings broke records with over 30,000 shareholders attending the meeting. It was so large that Dhirubhai had to book a football field to fit everyone.

With such a meteoric rise to the top, Dhirubhai stepped on many toes to get to where he was. He wanted to be number one. Being number two, as he often told his team, was not good enough. He countered every charge of corruption, political manipulation, and breaking the law with characteristic, irrefutable, bold moves. No matter what he was accused of, he could do no wrong in the eyes of his shareholders. He had made them richer than they could have imagined.

When Dhirubhai died in 2002, he left behind a multinational conglomerate, with a turnover of nearly ₹600 billion, making him a billionaire several times over. In 2016, he was posthumously awarded the Padma Vibhushan.

He had not only kept his promise to his mother but also changed the way the common man invests his money. His legacy continues to grow and expand with time.

14

NAMBI NARAYANAN

The Scientist Who Defied the Odds

The whole of India was transfixed, watching with bated breath as the spacecraft successfully landed on the moon after a 40-day journey in space. Cheers erupted and a billion people celebrated. Chandrayaan-3 was a success. It was a huge moment in Indian aerospace exploration. What few realized was that behind the power and success of the Chandrayaan spacecraft was an engine called Vikas. If it wasn't for this engine, Chandrayaan might never have taken off. And neither would India's ambitious space programme.

The Vikas engine was the brainchild of a scientist named Nambi Narayanan. Sadly for Narayanan, it wasn't Vikas that he became famous for. It was a set of circumstances that painted him as a spy who sold his nation's secrets to enemy countries, attracting the attention of the world. This charge against him was dropped, as it was proved false. Narayanan went on to become a celebrated scientist, winning awards and recognition. That, though, wasn't how life started out for him.

A Math Prodigy

Nambi Narayanan was born on 12 December 1941 in a tiny village in Nagercoil in Tamil Nadu. He had four elder sisters. His father earned his living as a small businessman, trading in coconut kernels and fibres. As a boy, Narayanan excelled in school. He loved mathematics and was fascinated by anything that flew. He topped his school in his board exams and went on to study engineering. When it was time to get a job, he joined a sugar factory. His job was to oversee the entire process—from sugarcane crushing to the end product. Narayanan tackled his job with his usual gusto. But his yearning for mathematics, rockets and airplanes never left him. He quit his job at the sugar factory and moved to Thiruvananthapuram. That's when fate took a hand in his life.

Destiny Intervenes

One day, he went to a store to pick up some groceries wrapped in a newspaper. He spotted an advertisement in the wrapper. The Thumba Equatorial Rocket Launching Station (TERLS) was inviting applications from engineers. Narayanan was immediately interested. This seemed right up his alley. The last date for applications was already over, but Narayanan went ahead and applied.

TERLS was operated by ISRO (Indian Space Research Organisation), led by the eminent scientist Vikram Sarabhai. A scientist in his team named Abdul Kalam (who later became the President of India) interviewed Narayanan. He found him eminently suitable for what they needed. On 12 September 1966, Narayanan joined India's first space exploration team. All thanks to a chance spotting of a newspaper carrying groceries.

As Narayanan found his feet in his new role, one area fascinated him. There were mixed views on whether the rockets they planned to build and send into space should be driven by solid- or liquid-fuelled engines. The technology available in India in those days made solid-fuelled engines more accessible. A majority of the team at ISRO was in favour of using solid-fuelled engines. It was a low-risk, quick-reward solution. But

Narayanan was not convinced.

'Why do most nations with advanced space exploration abilities use liquid-fuelled engines?' he wondered. He set about trying to figure it out. During this time, he won a scholarship to Princeton University in the USA. He completed his degree in ten months instead of the two years it would normally take. The Americans saw in him tremendous potential and tried to convince him to stay back.

But Vikram Sarabhai, who had been mentoring him, wanted him on his team. ISRO had ambitious plans, and Narayanan had just what it took to be part of the team. Back in India, Narayanan focused on developing his pet project: a liquid-propelled engine that he strongly believed would help India's space programme move forward faster.

The Birth of Vikas

Together with his team, Narayanan built a liquid-propelled engine that had a thrust of 600 kg. But that was nothing compared to what the Americans and Russians, who were in a fierce space war, were using. Their liquid-propelled engines had a thrust of 60 tonnes—100 times more than what the ISRO team had developed. This would not do for Narayanan.

He put his team on the task. He collaborated with the French, who were on a similar journey as India. After months of trials, the team, led by Narayanan, was successful in building a liquid-propelled engine that had a thrust of 60 tonnes, at par with the best in the world. He named his engine Vikas.

Vikas meant progress. But Narayanan had another reason for choosing this name. It was also a somewhat modified acronym for Vikram A. Sarabhai—his mentor and guru. The Vikas engine now made it possible to launch heavier space vehicles thanks to its vastly superior thrust. In October 1994, a PSLV (Polar Satellite Launch Vehicle) was successfully launched into space, much to the delight of ISRO scientists. The Indian space programme led by ISRO now had wings. There were over 50 such launches, which went smoothly thanks to the 'stubborn' Vikas engine, which never seemed to give up.

A Shocking Turn of Events

Narayanan's career was now firmly on track as an aerospace scientist. He was a trusted and valued member of ISRO. But things were about to get very ugly.

In November 1994, three policemen knocked at Narayanan's door. Without any explanation, they took him to the police station, telling him only that they were 'questioning' him. A puzzled Narayanan spent the entire night in the lock-up, wondering why he had been brought there.

The next day, he was produced in court and the judge asked him if he had sold technology to Pakistan. Narayanan was even more mystified as he had done nothing of the sort. He finally understood the case against him. He was being accused of passing on 'secret drawings and papers' of the technology developed at ISRO to Pakistan through some Maldivian women, who Narayanan was accused of knowing.

Narayanan was completely at sea. He had no knowledge of any Maldivian women. He had never even discussed anything confidential with anyone outside ISRO. For the next few months, Narayanan's life was a living hell. He was charged with violating India's official secrets law. He was accused of being corrupt. His reputation was in tatters. He was interrogated for hours, sometimes beaten and chained to a bed. He was imprisoned alongside serial killers. But throughout this traumatic period, Narayanan held to his innocence. He argued his case, insisting that rocket secrets and drawings could not be 'transferred to a piece of paper'. He was, he claimed, without a doubt being framed.

Exonerated at Last

A month after his arrest, the Central Bureau of Investigation (CBI) took over the case. When their investigations didn't yield a single piece of evidence to support the case against Narayanan, he was exonerated. In 1998, the Supreme Court dismissed the case.

Narayanan was proven innocent. But the trauma he and his family suffered angered him. He sued the Kerala government and was awarded ₹5 million in compensation. For Narayanan, it wasn't the money that mattered. He wanted to tell the world that when you are innocent, there is nothing to fear and that you must fight back. Till today, no one knows who was behind the framing. There are theories, but none has been proven.

Narayanan went back to ISRO, where he continued his groundbreaking work. He retired in 2001. In 2019, he was awarded the Padma Bhushan for his contribution to science. A movie, *Rocketry: The Nambi Effect*, was made on his life to great appreciation.

Nambi Narayanan's contribution to India's space efforts opened up the universe, proving the sky is really not the limit.

15

RAKESH SHARMA

A Journey into Space

Rakesh Sharma had been locked up for three days in a room with no windows, no natural light, and no fresh air. But he wasn't worried, for this was a test to see if he could handle being confined in these conditions for long periods. Only then could he move to the next stage of his journey—one which would take him closer to achieving his dream of going into space and exploring its mysteries.

A dream that he fulfilled. But before reaching his goal, he had a long and arduous road to travel.

A Young Techie

Even as a child, Rakesh loved technology and electronics. When he was just a teenager, his family and friends would seek his help in fixing electronic devices, even though he had no training in it. It's no wonder, then, that this young man, with his determination and talent, would reach for the skies—literally.

Sharma was born on 13 January 1949 in Patiala. His family moved to Hyderabad, where he attended school and college. He joined the National Defence Academy and then the Air Force. The flying bug had bitten him, and he was never happier than when he was conquering the skies.

In 1971, during the war against Pakistan, Sharma flew over 20 combat missions as Squadron Leader in a MiG-21 fighter jet, overcoming the enemy. His bravery and skill were recognized by the authorities. Sharma went on to become Wing Commander.

Ready to Take off

It was in September of 1982 that Sharma's dream really took off. He was selected from hundreds to become a cosmonaut and go into space as part of a joint space programme with the Soviets. The Soviet leader at the time was a man named Leonid Brezhnev, who had grand ambitions to explore the mysteries of outer space. India, too, was gearing up for one such mission. At the time, Indira Gandhi was the Prime Minister of India. The two leaders collaborated and decided to send a joint mission to explore space.

The Indian Air Force was asked to select two candidates for the mission. Sharma's skill and courage had not gone unnoticed. He was selected along with another airman, named Ravish Malhotra. One of them would eventually get the opportunity to go into space. The other was to be a backup in case something went wrong. Two Russian cosmonauts would also be a part of the mission.

A Tough Training

Going into space is not for the faint-hearted. Sharma and Malhotra embarked on a gruelling training schedule. Not only did they have to be physically fit, they also needed to be mentally prepared for what was coming.

First, the duo went through technical training to understand every nuance of their spaceship. There were no mechanics in space to help them if they encountered a mechanical snag.

Next, they had to prepare their bodies for what was to come. The training was intense. In outer space, all kinds of unexpected things can happen to the human body. There is zero gravity in space. The body takes up to 72 hours to get used to this condition. Blood rushes to the head. The face and tongue can develop ulcers. Drowsiness, headaches, nausea and motion sickness may occur. The absence of gravity can make a person feel very unwell. Sharma and Malhotra had already been through the early test of being locked in a room for three days to see if they were claustrophobic.

Sharma was determined not to let anything deter him. He had been preparing in his own way. He began to practise yoga. This helped him later when he was in space.

He passed all the preliminary tests. Now it was time to go to the next stage. Sharma and Malhotra were sent to Russia for further, even more intensive, training. Russia was a whole new world. It was freezing with temperatures well below zero degrees. Sharma had never experienced that kind of cold before.

'We had to walk in freezing cold from one building to another,' recounts Sharma, thinking back to those days. Not only that, but the training was also conducted entirely in Russian. So he had to learn Russian first. He would practise Russian for as many as six to seven hours every day.

In three months, he had learnt enough Russian to understand the training commands easily. The training went on for two long years. Finally Sharma, Malhotra and the two Russian cosmonauts were declared ready for the mission. Their training had enhanced their endurance, their strength, and above all, their ability to adapt to different conditions. It was as if they were preparing for the Olympics but with perhaps more at stake. For Sharma, it was about taking his country into an unconquered frontier.

A Life-Changing Experience

Finally, the big day arrived. Though both cosmonauts were fully prepared, it was Sharma who was chosen. Malhotra was disappointed, but also happy for his mate. He hugged him and wished him luck.

'All the best, my friend,' he said. 'This is your chance to make India proud.' Sharma was armed with the good wishes and love of every Indian. And fortified with *suji halwa, aloo chole,* and pulao—dishes he took with him, to remind him of home.

The launch facility from which the rocket was to take off was in modern-day Kazakhstan, concealed in the backwoods of the Union of Soviet Socialist Republics (USSR). The Russians were in a space race with the

USA and wanted to keep this launch under wraps until it happened. On 3 April 1984, the spaceship Soyuz T-11 was launched. On board were Rakesh Sharma, Yury Malyshev and Gennady Strekalov, the three cosmonauts who were set to make history.

Was Sharma nervous? Not a bit! They had practised the entire process a million times before, so it seemed like just another practice.

The Final Frontier

The spacecraft shot into space. Soon, the deafening sound of the spaceship travelling through the Earth's atmosphere was replaced by the deathly silence of space. The Earth became smaller and smaller, and black nothingness enveloped it. As the spacecraft shot through the Earth's atmosphere, the force of gravity went on building up until it suddenly dropped to zero.

Sharma and the other cosmonauts could see the Earth. They all tried to spot their own country. Sharma took a deep breath, his heart pounding. And then he saw it. The coastlines. The forests. The deserts. The mountains. India. His India. The country he was taking to the forefront of space exploration.

Sharma heaved a sigh. The feeling he had was like nothing he had experienced before. He saw the beauty of his home planet. He felt the exhilaration of being in space. He felt the smallness of the human race. He experienced the universe in all its magnificence and vastness. This was something that very few people in the world could experience. Sharma was humbled.

The crew spent 7 days, 21 hours and 40 minutes on board the spacecraft. As they orbited Earth, they had work to do. They conducted over 40 experiments, with Sharma focusing on biomedicine and remote sensing. The information they gathered would change the course of science for decades to come.

When Sharma returned from his hugely successful mission, he was received with appreciation, awards and adulation—and questions.

'Did you meet God in outer space?' a woman is said to have asked him. While still in space, Sharma spoke to Indira Gandhi, who asked him how India looked from outer space. His famous reply was, '*Saare jahaan se achcha!*' (Better than the whole universe).

Sharma's achievement was India's achievement. He went on to win many recognitions. Among them were the Hero of the Soviet Union and the highest peacetime gallantry award—the Ashoka Chakra. But for him, the moment he saw his home planet from space was the most special of all. A moment he would never forget as long as he lived.

16

Kiran Bedi

Marching to a Different Beat

The year was 1975. Kiran Bedi looked right towards the Indian Prime Minister, Indira Gandhi, saluting as she marched. She was leading the Delhi Police Contingent in the Republic Day march, one of India's grandest and most prestigious spectacles. She was the first woman to do so. She was, in fact, the first woman to do many things because that's who she was. Determined, undaunted, and fiercely patriotic, Bedi loved to take challenges head-on. It's what drove her to go where no one had been before, becoming India's first woman to join the prestigious Indian Police Service (IPS).

Early Life Lessons

Kiran Bedi was born in 1949 in the well-to-do Peshwaria family in Amritsar. She was the second of four sisters. Born soon after Independence, she grew up at a time when people felt a great sense of patriotism towards their newly formed country. Mahatma Gandhi and Jawaharlal Nehru were national heroes. Every evening at dinner, the family would discuss values like tolerance, sacrifice and self-reliance.

Young Kiran was a lucky girl. Her parents didn't have the attitude that many had at that time—that marriage was the ultimate goal for all women. Her father encouraged his four daughters to study and follow their passion. Her mother emphasized the importance of never depending on others.

Although the family was well-off, Kiran's grandfather was from the old school of thought. When Kiran's eldest sister was admitted to a convent school, he was so angry that he cut off her family allowance, which was her father's share. Disturbed, but determined not to let anything come in the way of his daughter's education, their father moved out of the sprawling family home. Money was tight after that. Kiran's parents made many sacrifices to ensure that their girls received the best. It's no wonder that for Kiran, her parents remained role models her entire life.

Young Kiran threw herself into studies with typical single-mindedness. When she reached the tenth standard, while choosing her subjects she was offered a subject known as 'household'. In this, she was told, she would learn how to run a household with all the skills she would need to become a good housewife. The idea chilled her to the bone. She couldn't see her future tied to a kitchen, cooking and cleaning for her family.

Off the Beaten Track

Bedi took her first bold decision to transfer to another school, where she could study the subjects she wanted. Always defying traditional expectations, she took part in many sports—from hurdles to long jump to marathon running. And of course tennis.

Kiran's father was a talented tennis player and played at the local club. Kiran had been playing tennis at the club since she was nine years old. By the time she was 13, she was competing at the regional level. When she was 16, she became the national junior tennis champion.

Sports was not enough for the feisty Kiran. She joined the National Cadet Corps (NCC). She loved being in uniform. She thrived in the tough schedule. She marched, learnt to fire a weapon, and soon proved her mettle when she became one of NCC's youngest platoon commanders.

Clearly, Kiran was not cut in the same mould as the traditional Indian woman. Fed up with the daily ritual of combing out her long hair and shampooing and caring for it, she went to the local barber one day.

'Cut it off,' she asked him. She got the 'boy's cut' as it was called back then, and it was her signature look for the rest of her life.

A New Path

One day, at the club she struck up a conversation with some people who were civil servants. When she heard about the nature of what they did, she decided she wanted to join the Indian Administrative Services. The desire to do something that would help her serve the nation ran deep in her.

Kiran decided to appear for the administrative services exam. A sense of justice and fair play was deeply ingrained in her, and she set her sights on joining the police force.

Around this time, Bedi met the man who would become her husband. She had always been determined that if she ever married, it would be on her own terms.

'I will only get married if I meet someone who will never stop me from following my career path,' she declared. Finding such a man at a time when most people were conventional was a tall order. Fortune, they say, favours the bold. And Kiran was nothing if not bold.

She found the perfect partner in Brij Bedi. He was also a tennis player and wholeheartedly supported her ambitions. The young couple embarked on a highly unusual marriage. Both husband and wife followed their own career paths with complete dedication—often living in different cities for months and years. Even when they had a daughter, Kiran kept her career at the forefront, with her parents and in-laws providing a strong support system.

It was time for the tough civil services examination. As with everything else she had tried so far, Kiran succeeded. She was now ready for the gruelling training schedule that would make her a full-fledged IPS officer. The only woman in a batch of 80, she aced her training too.

Kiran Bedi had arrived. She was finally ready to join the police force.

Time for Action

It was during her very first posting in Delhi that the newly appointed IPS officer Kiran Bedi got a taste of what life was going to be like.

The date was 5 November 1979. Things were tense because a simmering clash had erupted between members of the Nirankari and Akali Sikhs due to differences in their beliefs. The police force was on alert, expecting violence to break out at any moment.

Rajpath, the ceremonial path that is the venue of India's Republic Day parade, was crowded. Hundreds of Akali Sikhs, swords in hand, marched furiously towards Rashtrapati Bhavan—the home of the President of India. As they approached, their fury reached a crescendo, and they charged forward with a war cry. The worst kind of violence was about to erupt.

Bedi reached there with her squad. Promptly, she sprang into action. Armed only with a baton and a helmet, she took the enraged crowd head-on. Blows rained down on her, but she stood steadfast beating them back. Intimidated by her sheer guts, the crowd abated. Her backup squad arrived, and things were brought under control. Breathing heavily, Bedi watched the crowd being dispersed. She had successfully quelled her first riot. Her act of bravery won her the Police Medal for Gallantry.

The wonderful thing about Bedi is not just that she was a fearless cop. She fought terrorists fearlessly; she changed the way inmates were treated in prisons; she worked to stop drug trafficking; and she also made sure that the policemen on night duty on freezing winter nights were given hot tea to keep the chill away.

It's no wonder that the name Kiran Bedi has inspired so many young women to follow their own dreams—and many to join the police force. She has helped change the way women and girls see themselves.

17

NARENDRA MODI

A Man on a Mission

Young Narendra deftly poured a glass of piping hot ginger tea for a waiting customer. His father's tiny tea stall at the railway station was a popular spot among the villagers. They would stop by to drink a quick cup of chai and exchange local news. Narendra loved to listen to the travellers as they chatted over a glass of chai. He was a thoughtful, observant young boy and these early interactions with people stayed with him, building in him the ability to connect with people from all strata of society. This was an important skill for the incredibly important office he was going to hold in the future, that of the Prime Minister of India.

A Curious Mind

Narendra Damodardas Modi was born on 17 September 1950 in the small, dusty town of Vadnagar—the third of six children. His parents, Damodardas and Hiraben, were simple, hardworking people. They were not very well off and had a large family to feed. The tea stall added to the meagre income. Vadnagar was a thriving little community with bustling markets and narrow alleys. The town was steeped in history and is said to have been a centre of Buddhist learning centuries ago.

The school Modi went to as a child was a basic one. The teachers did the best they could with their limited resources. They had a willing pupil in the young Modi. He was a curious and thoughtful lad, different from boys his age. He was deeply interested in philosophy, loved debates, and had endless questions about life.

India at this time was still finding its feet as a newly independent nation. There were many debates and conversations about development, social justice, and national identity. Modi, who spent many hours in the school library, was keenly interested in all the discussions he heard around him. A voracious reader, he had come across the writings of Swami Vivekananda and was inspired by him. When he was eight years old, he attended his first Rashtriya Swayamsevak Sangh (RSS) meeting. RSS is an organization that is committed to building and retaining the cultural values of the country. He became a *balswayamsevak*, or a junior volunteer. It was here that Modi imbibed not just the physical discipline that would stay with him his entire life, but also an enduring sense of duty to the community and the nation.

In Quest of Answers

By the time he was 17, Modi's thirst for knowledge was too much to ignore. He left home and decided to travel across India to get to know his country better. For two years, he wandered the length and breadth of the country. He bathed in freezing Himalayan waters. He met saints and sadhus at railway stations, followed them around, asking them questions about spirituality. When he returned home, he was a changed man. He believed he had found his calling. He wanted to dedicate his life to his country. He wanted to help those in need. And he wanted the Indian people to find their own identity and be proud of it, after centuries of colonial rule.

In 1970, Modi went to Ahmedabad. He became a full-time member of the RSS, while also working in his uncle's canteen. The strict routine of waking at dawn, spartan meals, and interactions with people on the ground gave him a deeper understanding of people and politics. He had proved himself to be a master organizer.

First Steps in Politics

Around this time, India was under a state of Emergency, declared by the then Prime Minister Indira Gandhi. During the Emergency, all fundamental rights of citizens were suspended. People were being jailed without explanation and the media was suppressed. Modi became a part of a committee formed to resist the Emergency. He went underground to avoid arrest, often disguised as a turbaned Sikh or a saffron-clothed sanyasi.

When the Emergency was lifted, Modi was put in charge of the Surat and Vadodara divisions of the RSS. His organizational abilities and skills as an impactful orator caught the eye of the higher-ups of the Bharatiya Janata Party (BJP), and in 1987, he was appointed the General Secretary of the Gujarat wing of the BJP. He rose through the ranks in the BJP, thanks to his incredible administrative abilities and his knack for connecting with people. In 1998, he was promoted to the position of national general secretary. The next few years saw internal squabbles within the party and in 2001, Modi found himself, quite suddenly, appointed as Chief Minister of Gujarat.

Narendra Modi the politician had arrived.

An Enduring Chief Minister

His years as Chief Minister were turbulent. A tragic earthquake devastated parts of the state and Modi had to deal with the terrible fallout. No sooner had he completed the relief and reconstruction measures than Gujarat was catapulted into the throes of communal riots. An attack on the Sabarmati Express resulted in the death of many passengers. Riots broke out and many people, both Hindus and Muslims, were killed. Modi was criticized and even blamed by the opposition and sections of the media for his handling of the riots. The Supreme Court of India, examining the issue, exonerated him.

Modi now turned to his main focus—development—an issue he was passionate about. Quick to act, he took several measures that hugely impacted Gujarat's progress. Roads and highways were built and improved, new public spaces were created, Gujarat became an easy place to do business, and the people began to prosper economically. Delighted with their new Chief Minister, they re-elected him again and again. He was CM of Gujarat for over 12 years.

Becoming Prime Minister

It was time for the 2014 general elections. This time Modi stood for election from Varanasi and Vadodara. He won both hands down. In May 2014, Narendra Modi was sworn in as the fourteenth Prime Minister of India.

Now Modi was finally in a position where he could impact his country's progress on a larger scale. He wasted no time in putting sweeping measures into place, some of which were criticized by naysayers. The nationwide GST (Goods and Services Tax), the crackdown on black money, a mission to build public toilets, helping the poorest have their bank accounts, providing cooking gas connections to villagers, promoting digital platforms to enable digital money transactions, these were all major initiatives that sought to improve the lives of the common man. Even though some of the measures were initially disruptive, people felt they were beneficial, and Modi once again led his party to victory, and became PM, in 2019.

The Covid Battle

Modi was barely into his second term as PM when the Covid-19 pandemic shut the world down. Businesses, small and big, came to a standstill. To curb the spread of the dreaded virus, Modi announced a nationwide lockdown. The economic costs were high, and Modi came in for major criticism from various quarters. Never one to back down from his convictions, Modi focused on developing a vaccine. A free vaccine, he believed, would be the answer to keeping over a billion Indians safe from the deadly virus.

He gave his full support to the scientists who were developing Covaxin, India's home-grown vaccine. He also smoothed the path for another vaccine, Covishield. At the same time, he put into place immediate relief measures, including free food for the poor across the nation, and making capital available to small businesses to tide them over this period.

To give the people of India confidence, he took the first jab of the Covaxin vaccine. The world's largest vaccination programme was implemented and over two billion doses were given to people across India. Not only that, but Modi also offered vaccine support to other affected countries. When Covid was finally over, the world acknowledged India and Modi's handling of the pandemic.

The Global Face of India

Modi was not done yet. From the moment he took oath as Prime Minister, he vowed to bring India onto the world stage as a serious player. From his very first speech at the United Nations, where he proudly spoke in Hindi, to his efforts to make India self-reliant with his *Atmanirbhar Bharat* (self-reliant India) programme, Modi took several unconventional steps towards building India's stature as a global player. He made several diplomatic visits to countries and invited world leaders to visit India. In 2022, as president of the G-20, an important global forum comprising 19 countries and the European Union as a bloc, India hosted a summit where 23 nations came together and discussed global issues.

After the next general election in 2024, Modi was once again sworn in as Prime Minister. At the moment of writing this, Modi is in the midst of his third term as Prime Minister. He has been acknowledged as one of the most influential people of this century. India today is a global force, and the world has taken note.

Modi has had his share of criticism and allegations. But his convictions remain strong. He believes there's a lot to be done. He remains one of India's most consequential prime ministers. A long way from a humble tea stall.

18

BACHENDRI PAL

The Woman Who Conquered the Mountains

Bachendri Pal looked at the vertical wall of ice in front of her. She, along with other climbers, was close to the summit of Mount Everest. It was freezing. Cold winds howled at a speed of 100 kilometres per hour. The temperature hovered between -30 degrees and -40 degrees celsius. Bachendri had to climb this frozen wall of ice to realize her dream.

Her mind went back to the days when, as a child, she roamed the hills and climbed mountains with her friends. She remembered the day so well when the idea of climbing Everest had first hit her. Her mind wandered for a moment to those early days of a simple but tough childhood.

Working Hard

Bachendri was born on 24 May 1954 in Nakuri, a tiny village in the Garhwal hills of Uttarakhand. Her father was a small-time businessman who supplied groceries to Tibet. The family was large and the income he brought in was simply not enough to provide for seven children. However, her parents were determined to ensure that their children received a good education.

Bachendri did her bit, helping around the house. One day, she discovered that her mother had sold her gold chain to earn some extra money. Bachendri's heart was heavy. She couldn't stand the thought of her parents working so hard, especially knowing that her mother had to sell her only cherished piece of jewellery. This made her sad. But it also made her determined to make all the sacrifices they had made worth it. She worked harder than ever—at her studies and at sport, at which she excelled.

Full of energy and enthusiasm, she gave the school her all. Bachendri's abilities and grit caught the principal's eye.

'This girl must be given every opportunity,' thought the principal. He made sure that Bachendri went to college for higher studies. She was the first girl in the village to do so.

The Call of the Mountains

Throughout her school years and even when she went to college, Bachendri was fascinated by the hills and mountains. As a child of the hills, the mountains held an almost godlike place in her heart. When she was just 12 years old, she and a few other intrepid friends decided to try their hand at mountaineering. They managed to scale a peak that was over 13,000 feet above sea level—a serious climb for a child.

Even though the mountains called to her, her education, for which her parents had sacrificed so much, could not wait. She focused on her studies and completed her master's as well as her BEd—a certification that qualified her as a teacher. Everyone was certain she would choose a teaching career, but the lure of the mountains was too much for Bachendri. She wanted to become a mountaineer.

In the face of disbelief and some derision from people around her, she trained at the Nehru Institute of Mountaineering (NIM) in Uttarkashi. And Bachendri was nothing if not determined. She was a dauntless climber and as her skills grew, so did her ambition.

Her first incredible milestone came during her course at the NIM. Her goal was the breathtaking Mount Gangotri, towering over 21,900 feet above the surrounding mountains. She had to cross miles of rocky moraines (material left behind by shifting glaciers), traverse a mighty glacier, and hike across loose snowfields before conquering the peak.

Her ability, attitude and skills did not go unnoticed. She was offered a job as an instructor at the National Adventure Foundation. She was now financially secure with a job she loved—a far cry from being a teacher at the local school.

The Final Summit

She felt it was time to test her limits. Her heart was set on climbing to the summit of Mount Everest, the highest mountain in the world. It wasn't just the climb that was challenging. It was also the conditions. Altitude sickness, breathing difficulties, dangerous wind speed, hazardous avalanches—these were just some conditions that had overwhelmed climbers over the years. Many lost their lives in pursuit of this ultimate challenge.

But Bachendri's heart was set on this. As she began preparations, she was met with much resistance.

'A woman? Climbing the Everest?' It was a refrain she often heard, but one that made her more determined than ever. After months of preparation, she was finally ready. In May 1984, Bachendri and her team began their adventure.

It was a mixed team of eleven men and six women. Divided into two, Bachendri was part of the forward team. On the night of 15 May, the forward team pitched camp at an altitude of 24,000 feet. They would stay the night here and proceed the next morning. It was 12:30 at night when Bachendri woke up with a jolt. There was a deafening crash, and moments later, the entire camp was engulfed by an enormous mass of snow. Pal was crushed under a cold, freezing pile of snow. She was convinced that this was the end. But fate had something else in store. She was pulled out of the snow by a team member who had broken free. But many others were not so lucky and were badly injured.

The team that was following behind was informed and rushed to help the injured. With such an enormous setback, the entire expedition was now in question. But Bachendri was determined.

'Those of us who are fine should go on,' she declared. 'We might never get another chance like this.' Many of the team decided to return to base camp. She was now the only woman in the smaller team to continue.

They restarted their climb. Braving the freezing wind that howled like a banshee around her, gritting her teeth against the merciless cold, and reaching into the innermost recesses of her willpower and strength, Bachendri forged on. And finally, on 23 May, she planted the Indian tricolour on the summit of the highest mountain on earth, Mount Everest, at an altitude of over 29,000 feet.

Success at Last

Bachendri was literally on top of the world. She had overcome hardships, scepticism and misogyny; she had fought against every obstacle—physical and social—and now she was here. The first Indian woman to scale the world's tallest mountain.

Her life changed after that. In 1984 she received the Padma Shri, and in 1986 the Arjuna Award, and her name appeared in the *Guinness Book of Records* as the first Indian woman to scale Mount Everest. More awards followed.

Bachendri continued her conquests of the mountains. Although she had conquered the highest of all mountains, she wanted to make this feat possible for other women climbers. In 1985, she led an all-women Indo-Nepalese expedition team, creating several new world records. She also went on to lead India's first women's trans-Himalayan expedition, crossing a gruelling 4,500-kilometre stretch through the deadly Siachen Glacier.

Today, Bachendri Pal stands tall not only for her Himalayan feat but also for her grit which helped her overcome almost impossible obstacles. She remains an inspiration to women and girls who want to break the mould and follow their dreams.

19

KAPIL DEV

The Haryana Hurricane

The lanky 16-year-old Kapil looked at the meagre two chapatis and dal on his plate with dismay. He was ravenous. He was at the Cricket Club of India's under-19 coaching camp and had bowled for more than four hours in the heat and humidity of Mumbai. He still had half a day's bowling ahead of him. He went up to the authorities.

'I am a fast bowler. I will need more food than this,' he said. The authorities just scoffed.

'Fast bowler? There are no fast bowlers in India, so don't give us that,' came the snarky response.

Kapil was upset with this taunt. He vowed to change

this perception. And he did. He not only proved them wrong but also became India's most celebrated fast bowler and all-rounder, feared by the best batters in the world.

Early Days

Kapil Dev Nikhanj was born on 6 January 1959 in Chandigarh, which was then part of the undivided state of Punjab. His father, Ram Lal Nikhanj, was a timber merchant. His family was comfortably well-off. As the second youngest of seven siblings, Kapil was everyone's pet. Kuckoo, as he was known, was always up to mischief. Although studies were not his forte, he excelled in every sport he took part in. He discovered the joy of cricket early in his life. His elder brother, Bhushan, recognizing his natural cricketing talent, encouraged him and signed him up for cricket coaching.

One day, Kapil's father overheard the cricket coach talking to Bhushan.

'Kapil has talent, but needs to build strength,' said the coach. The next thing the family knew, there were two buffaloes in the backyard, that Kapil's father had bought, to ensure that Kapil had enough fresh milk to build up his strength.

With wholehearted support from his family, and his own talent and grit, it was no surprise that Kapil caught the eye of the cricketing world. Indian cricket, in those days, was dominated by batting geniuses and spin bowlers. Having an Indian fast bowler of a high calibre seemed almost beyond imagination.

In 1978, India and Pakistan played a benefit match for a retired cricketer. The Pakistani fast bowlers, larger than life, glanced at a nervous young Kapil. When he was introduced as a fast bowler, the Pakistani cricketers smirked, saying, 'So now India is going to produce fast bowlers?'

Kapil made them regret their words when, just a few years later, he took 32 wickets during a six-match Test series against Pakistan, becoming the youngest player to cross the twin milestones of 1,000 runs and 100 wickets.

Kapil Dev, the fast bowler and all-rounder, had truly arrived.

Thus began Kapil Dev's blitzkrieg. His free-spirited batting and natural bowling made him the hero of Indian fans. His aggressive, never-say-die spirit permeated Indian cricket, giving them a self-belief they didn't have before.

In the years from 1978 to 1983, Kapil Dev stormed the Indian cricket scene. There were many jaw-dropping, match-winning performances. His five wickets for 28 runs against Australia in Melbourne in 1981, his nine wickets haul against the West Indies in 1983, his attacking game, and his indefatigable energy earned him the nickname 'The Haryana Hurricane'.

But his biggest moment was yet to come. In 1983, just 24 years old, Dev was made the captain of the India team, to lead them in the Prudential World Cup in England, and he was fiercely determined to put down all the naysayers who had been scoffing at India's chances.

The 'No-Hope' Team

The Indian team arrived in England as clear underdogs, some even calling them the 'no-hope' team. They had to face seven countries, including the ruthless West Indians, the canny English, and the powerful Australians. It was an impossible task. The Indian team had a poor ODI record, especially when it came to World Cup matches.

The world cricketing fraternity scoffed at India's chances. 'If India wins, I will eat my words,' a British journalist famously declared. All these snide comments made Dev even more determined. In the very first match of the World Cup, India was up against the mighty juggernaut of the West Indies team. Although it was not a knockout match, it set the tone for India's campaign when to everyone's astonishment, India won.

Match after match, the Indian team made their way to the finals, as the rest of the world watched in disbelief. Dev kept the morale high, leading from the front.

A Turning Point

It was a critical match against Zimbabwe, a team that was not considered one of the top-order teams. When Dev came out to bat, India were nine runs for four wickets, a disaster in the making. To the horror of the Indian fans, another wicket fell for just 17 runs. Defeat was certain and with it, any hope of making it even to the semi-finals. Dev looked around. He studied the field. He took a deep breath. And he did what he did best. He hit! Hard! He went on a rampage, making 175 not out, winning the pivotal match for India.

Stunned spectators looked on. The tragedy is that this match was considered so insignificant that the media did not even cover it. Yet, it became a turning point for India's World Cup campaign.

The Final Face-Off

In an unbelievable turn of events, India was in the finals, facing the furious West Indies team, who were raring to take revenge on the mild-mannered Indians. The West Indians were known for their intimidation tactics and there was much jeering and booing as the Indian team walked onto the field, bowling first.

The West Indies had a formidable batting line-up, with icons like Gordon Greenidge, Clive Lloyd and Vivian Richards leading the attack. After losing an early wicket, the West Indies team picked up pace. But far from being intimidated, Dev called on his inner fighter. When Richards was lured to hit a six, Dev ran backward almost 20 metres to scoop up an almost impossible catch, dismissing Richards.

That was the beginning of the end for the West Indies. From a comfortable score of 50/2, the team collapsed when a buoyant Dev and his men hammered them, bowling them all out for a mere 140. Winning the World Cup in 1983 is now part of cricket lore. Indian cricket history is divided into 'before 1983 and after 1983'.

Kapil Dev's statistics are proof of his effort, grit and determination. By the time he retired from cricket in 1994, he held the world record for most wickets in Test matches, a record he held for many years until Courtney Walsh broke it in 2000. He is the first player to have taken 200 ODI wickets, the only player to have taken over 400 wickets (434 to be precise), and he has scored over 5,000 runs in Test cricket, making him quite simply India's greatest all-rounder. He started the 'fast-bowling revolution' in Indian cricket, inspiring many youngsters to become fast bowlers.

In 2002, Kapil Dev was named 'Indian cricketer of the century' by *Wisden*, cricket's most respected publication. In 2010, he was inducted into the ICC Cricket Hall of Fame.

So many years on, Kapil Dev remains in a league of his own.

20

KRISHNA ELLA

The Vaccine Superhero

As a little boy, Krishna watched his parents working tirelessly in the fields, his mother balancing the demands of labour, home, and caring for her eight children with quiet strength. Krishna absorbed the lesson that nothing can be achieved without hard work and determination. This belief took root in him, fuelling a relentless drive that would come to define his life.

That same persistence carried Ella far beyond the fields of his childhood. He rose to become a pioneering scientist, a champion of public health, and a vaccine innovator whose work would save millions. In the face of a global pandemic, Ella's leadership became India's hope for self-reliance, as he stood at the forefront of the nation's fight against the dreaded virus.

A Farmer First

Krishna Ella was born in 1969 in a tiny village in Tamil Nadu, into a family of farmers. He was the youngest of eight children. Living in a small village, Krishna did not have many distractions, like television or computers. He spent a lot of time with nature, observing life around him.

There were no really good schools in their village. So, Krishna moved to Chennai when he was in eighth grade. He was only the second in his family to get an education. With his farming background, he decided to learn more about agriculture. After finishing school, he got his degree in agricultural sciences in Bangalore. He returned home and told his father he wanted to start farming.

'What do you know about farming?' his father enquired.

'Well, I have a degree in agricultural science,' Ella told him proudly.

'That is a piece of paper,' his father scoffed. 'What do you know about cropping, managing labour, wheat control, rain and sun? Get a job instead. That is what your degree is for.'

Reluctantly, Ella joined the pesticides division of Bayer, a multinational pharmaceutical and biomedical company. He spent several years in the corporate world, first at Bayer and then at Sandoz, another multinational pharma company. It was around this time he married Suchitra, who became a major influence in his life.

A New Phase

Suchitra, an economics graduate, believed her husband was made for greater accomplishments. She encouraged him to apply to universities abroad and study further. Ella did not have enough money to pay for a foreign education. Luckily, he received a fellowship from the Rotary Foundation, which funded his higher education. This time, he chose microbiology, a decision that would change his life.

After completing his master's degree, he went on to do his PhD and then worked as a research faculty member at a leading medical university. This is where his mind opened to the immense possibilities of gene knockout technology, which helped Ella to develop vaccines. The more he studied viruses and virology, the more excited he became about the possibilities he could see in preventing and curing diseases. During this period, he nurtured a vision of finding novel solutions to tackle neglected diseases affecting developing nations.

But the call of home was too strong to ignore, especially for his wife Suchitra.

'We are foreigners in this country,' she said to him. 'We should go back to India, where you can put your new skills to good use.'

Back Home

Ella agreed, and in 1996 they returned home to India. They renounced their US citizenship and became Indian citizens. Now the question was, what to do? Starting a business needed capital. Feeling unsure about the huge step they had taken, they got into a family huddle.

'Don't worry, son,' said Ella's mother. 'We will sell our land if you need money. But you go ahead and follow your dream.'

That was all the motivation Ella needed. Together with Suchitra, he started the company Bharat Biotech with the aim of using his skills to develop healthcare solutions that even the poorest could afford, and to fight dreaded diseases that could, in the future, turn into pandemics.

Tasting Success

At first, Ella conceptualized a safe and affordable vaccine to fight hepatitis B, a virus that attacked the liver and killed many in India. A single vaccine during this period cost ₹4,000, an amount the common man could not easily afford, let alone the poor. Ella innovated a world-class, safe vaccine that was less expensive so that more people could afford it. But to execute a project like this on a large scale and produce enough vaccines would require significant investment.

He approached many investors to fund his startup and his vision, but they all turned him down, not believing that a small entrepreneur based out of India could compete with the big pharma companies that made and sold these vaccines. Ella was unfazed. He took loans, put in his own money, and went ahead and implemented the project.

He introduced the hepatitis B vaccine at an affordable price of ₹40, which was way below the expensive vaccine that cost ₹4,000. The world took notice.

Buoyed by this first success, Ella began to look for his next project. He had been watching with distress that many children in India were dying of diarrhoea, especially in the poorer sections of society. His research had revealed that the main cause of diarrhoea was rotavirus. He set to work and developed a vaccine to counteract the effects of the dreaded virus. He did large-scale efficacy trials to ensure his vaccine worked. When it was rolled out, it saved millions of children, not just in India, but also in Africa, Pakistan and other countries where the virus was rampant.

Ellas' successes after this came quick and fast. His company became the first in the world to develop vaccines against the dreaded chikungunya and Zika viruses. Farming being close to his heart, Ella also developed vaccines to save cattle and support farmers. His work was published in important science journals around the world. The World Health Organization (WHO) took his suggestions and predictions seriously.

Today, his company owns 220 patents and has delivered over nine billion vaccines and helped people in over 125 countries with its products.

The Real Challenge

But Ella's real challenge was just around the corner.

In 2019, a deadly virus called coronavirus was discovered in China. On 11 March 2020, the WHO declared it a pandemic. No country was spared as the lethal virus spread rapidly from person to person. The world came to a standstill.

Ella watched the spread with alarm, but also with some optimism and hope. He had been preparing for just such an eventuality. He was eager to contribute to India's efforts in becoming self-reliant, which was the need of the hour. As a virologist, he had long believed that it was only a matter of time before a pandemic swept the world. In anticipation, he had built BSL 3 production facilities. These facilities were built with the highest levels of containment measures, enabling the development of preventive vaccines against high-risk, dangerous pathogens. Further, there were mechanisms monitoring the spread of emerging and reemerging infectious diseases, ensuring better public health response.

Ella had already developed the indigenous Covaxin, which was safe and generated significant immunity against coronavirus and was in stage 3 of human trials, covering over 26,000 people.

But time was short as people were succumbing to the illness in huge numbers. Clinical trials typically took years. With his deep-rooted belief in working hard, Ella and his team worked tirelessly around the clock to develop and manufacture the vaccine.

Covaxin—after fast tracked, yet extensive, trials and much debate—proved to be safe and reported an 81% efficacy. It received regulatory approval and Prime Minister Narendra Modi took the first jab, giving the country much-needed confidence. Covaxin went on to become India's first indigenously developed and produced safe vaccine and was rolled out through the world's largest vaccination drive. Millions of Indians were vaccinated with Covaxin and it was also exported to many other countries. Many believe that it was Covaxin that turned the tide of Covid-19 in India.

Widely known as the father of the Genome Valley in Hyderabad, Krishna Ella won several national and international awards, including India's prestigious civilian award Padma Bhushan. His accomplishments include the creation of the Genome Valley in Hyderabad, driving the development of over 100 knowledge-based biotech companies around Bharat Biotech.

But his real reward is seeing children get ideas by observing the world around them. Innovation, he says, is not born through science. It is born through ideas. His next focus is improving the lives of farmers, because they, he believes, are the true entrepreneurs.

Ella's journey, from humble beginnings of rural hardship to the heights of international acclaim, is a shining example of the power of perseverance and vision.

21

VISWANATHAN ANAND

The Master of Moves

What cricket is to India, chess is to Russia. For years and years, Russia has dominated the world of chess. The idea that an Indian chess player could overthrow their grandmaster and become a world chess champion was unimaginable. And that too someone so young! Yet, that is precisely what happened when Viswanathan Anand stormed onto the world chess stage and ushered in a whole new era in Indian and world chess.

Early Promise

Even as a young boy, Vishy, as he was known, kept all the promise of becoming a chess wizard. Born on 11 December 1969 in Madras (now Chennai), he was the youngest of three children. His brother and sister were much older than him, so Anand found himself at home a lot with just his mother for company.

When he was six years old, his mother introduced him to chess. She was interested in the game herself and immediately spotted Anand's abilities. She became his first coach. Soon Anand began to beat her quite easily.

'It's time to get him proper coaching,' she decided. She began to look around for options.

One day, Anand's sister came home from college looking very excited. She had seen a sign for a chess club on her way back. As it turned out, the Mikhail Tal Chess Club (named after a Russian world chess champion) had regular coaches and tournaments. Anand started hanging around the club, watching games. He felt awkward and shy, not knowing if he should ask if he could play or if he needed to be invited. Although he was still young, his mother got his name included in the club's weekend tournaments. Anand didn't win his first tournament, but he got his first taste of serious chess. And he loved it.

When Anand was just over eight years old, his father was posted to Manila in the Philippines. Quite by chance, a much-celebrated World Chess Championship match between two world chess greats had just been held there, and the country was in the grip of a chess frenzy. Anand's mother found him a chess coach and enrolled him in a chess club. He got plenty of opportunities to practise chess and took part in many local tournaments.

A Winning Spree

Anand came back to Madras when he was eleven. His parents decided he should play tennis. He hated it. His tennis lessons came to a standstill, but his chess sped up. He began to top the five-minute blitz games that were usually played at the club. This was speed chess. As per the rules of this format, the winner was allowed to keep their place at the table, while the ones who lost had to go back to the end of a long queue. Anand was so good at this quick format that he ended up sitting for long periods at the table while his opponents came and went in quick succession.

Anand kept getting better and better at his game. His winning spree had just begun. In 1983, he won the National Sub-Junior Championship. The wins came rapidly after that—the National Junior Championship in 1984 and the Asian Junior Championship in 1985. Only two years later, at the age of 14, Anand became national champion. And finally, at the age of 18, he became India's first chess grandmaster.

Anand's mother had instilled a rather unique habit in him. She insisted that he made notes after each game. What he did right, and more importantly, what he did wrong. This became such a habit that he began to note down the smallest detail: opponents' gestures, things that distracted him, what helped him. He wrote little notes to himself like *'Don't get into any small talk. Stop making jokes and pretending to be funny.'* These notes became almost a manual and helped him at critical moments throughout his career.

The Big League

Viswanathan Anand was now a global name, and he had entered the big league. He needed to live closer to the places where international tournaments were held. He decided to shift base to Europe. He made his home in Spain, in a small place called Collado Mediano. He began the next quest in his chess journey: the world championship.

The 1990s were a tough period for Anand. After achieving his dream of becoming a grandmaster, he went through a low period, feeling a sense of emptiness as he had achieved his immediate goal. Throughout the 1990s, he crossed swords with the great Garry Kasparov and Vladimir Kramnik for the top slot. His first shot at the FIDE (Fédération Internationale des Échecs, the international chess federation) ended in a loss, although he reached the quarter-finals of the World Chess Championship cycle in 1993 and 1994–95.

His first international win came in Tehran in 2000, when he defeated Alexei Shirov in a match that lasted four days. But somehow Anand did not feel a sense of triumph. Many in the chess world called his win a fluke and did not acknowledge the format in which he had won as bonafide. There were critics of the short format and quick time controls used in the tournament. The powers that be in the chess world did not recognize Anand as world champion, even though he had beaten the top-seed Shirov.

Anand's dream was still unfulfilled.

The Final Frontier

The year was 2007 and the FIDE World Chess Championship was underway in Mexico City. It was a double round-robin tournament, which meant that each contestant had to play two games—one with white and one with black pieces—against every other player. Kramnik, who was the accepted 'classical champion' as acknowledged by FIDE, was Anand's chief opponent.

Recalling every bit of his past notes, observing every facial movement of his opponent, being mindful of his own giveaways and tells that might alert his opponent to what he was thinking, and keeping the element of surprise with him, Anand made his final move. Kramnik was forced to concede. The world had a new champion. Viswanathan Anand was the world champion.

He had won nine out of 14 points, had a total of four wins and 10 draws, and was the only unbeaten player in the tournament. His victory was total and undisputed. He was finally a world champion, just as he wanted to be.

He went on to win more world championships after this, in 2008, 2010 and 2012. Over the years, he won many tournaments in all forms of the game, whether classical, rapid or blitz. There was no reputed tournament in which he had not played, and no reputed player he had not defeated.

He outmanoeuvred the best, rattled champions, and bested opponents with his blitzkrieg.

Quite apart from his chess triumphs, he was awarded the Arjuna Award in 1985, the Padma Shri in 1987, the Padma Bhushan in 2000, and the Padma Vibhushan in 2007.

Viswanathan Anand inspired many youngsters in India to take up chess. His efforts have helped India produce several grandmasters and positioned the country as a serious contender on the world chess stage. Notwithstanding his achievements, when you think of Viswanathan Anand, a serious, mild, humble young man comes to mind, looking intently at the chessboard and planning his next move.

22

AMISH TRIPATHI
The Wondrous Wordsmith

A long queue of fans waited to get their copy signed by their favourite author, Amish Tripathi. There were eager students, starry-eyed professionals, hopeful future authors, and amid them, an old woman—a slightly unlikely reader of Amish's books. Amish spotted her and beckoned her to come in front of the crowd. The old lady stepped forward, beaming.

'I just want to bless you, son,' she said. 'I haven't read your books, but my grandchildren, who didn't know a thing about Indian culture, are suddenly interested in our history and our mythology. They have begun to pray. It's thanks to your books. So, I just wanted to meet you and tell you that.' The woman blessed a bemused Amish and left.

That interaction with the old woman stayed in Amish's mind. It's what gave him the most satisfaction when he looked back to his journey as a writer, during which he wrote 11 books, and sold over seven million copies worldwide that have been translated into over 20 languages. But becoming a writer—a bestselling one at that—was far from his mind in his rather austere childhood and youth.

An Austere Childhood

Amish and his twin brother Ashish, born on 18 October 1974, were the youngest of four siblings. Their parents came from modest families who placed great value on education. Amish's grandparents believed in the power of education and his parents were highly educated. It was no wonder that Amish and his brothers and sisters were encouraged not only to study but also to always strive for the best in everything they did.

If there was one thing Amish's family lacked in those early days, it was money. His parents, hugely knowledgeable and talented though they were, didn't know English. This was a challenge they faced throughout their lives. It made them determined that none of their children should ever have to go through the ignominy of not knowing English. They decided to send all four children to the most elite English schools so that they could master the language, learn from the best, and confidently hold their own with anyone, anywhere in the world.

After a stint as a boarder at St Lawrence School in Ooty, Amish found himself in an elite Mumbai school—the Cathedral and John Connon School. The shoes his classmates wore cost more than his father's salary. His mother was not allowed to enter the gate because the security guard thought she was a domestic maid. But far from making him self-conscious, this made him more determined to be worthy of the enormous sacrifices his parents made for their children.

A Diet of Culture and Mythology

Although their academic focus was on becoming proficient in English and getting the best education, at home the unrelenting focus was on keeping Indian traditions alive. With his father coming from a family of pandits, the love and respect for Indian mythology and the scriptures ran deep. Tales from the Ramayana and the Mahabharata were part of the bedtime stories. And dinner-table conversations revolved around discussions on philosophy, the Vedas, and the Upanishads. This deep knowledge of Indian history and mythology was to play an enormous part in shaping Amish's destiny later in life.

After completing school and college at St Xavier's College in Mumbai, Amish joined the Indian Institute of Management in Kolkata and obtained a degree in business management. With the monetary struggles his parents had faced all their lives still fresh in his mind, Amish decided to put his degree to use, get a stable job, and earn some money. For the next several years, he worked in the financial industry, building a decent financial foundation.

A Book is Born

But somewhere inside him, the fascination for Indian history, culture and mythology ran deep. Amish had once toyed with the idea of becoming a historian. So, he decided to write a book alongside his job. The book was to be a philosophical thesis on the nature of evil.

'A book with a story will be much more interesting,' Amish's brother suggested. 'Make it like an adventure.'

Amish thought about it. It seemed like a great idea. And so, he took Shiva as the protagonist. He built on the idea of Shiva being the destroyer of evil, and through Shiva's story, he shared his philosophies. A story, derived from India's great tradition of storytelling, was born. And in 2010, Amish's first book *The Immortals of Meluha* came to life.

However, Amish hadn't quite planned it that way. He wrote for himself and his family. He had no idea this would become a published book. The story took hold of him. He worked all day at the office and wrote all night—sometimes even at traffic signals. Finally, his first draft was ready. That's when he decided to try to get it published.

Facing Rejection

Amish approached publishers and showed them his manuscript. But he was rejected. Publisher after publisher turned him down, giving him reasons that didn't make sense to him at all.

'The subject isn't good enough. The book is too long.'

'This kind of stories don't sell in India.'

'Try writing an office romance with some scandal.'

'Write instead about how poor India is, write about its slums.'

'Your book has too much *gyaan* and philosophy. Dumb it down and we might consider it.'

But Amish didn't agree with this. He didn't want to dumb it down. He respected his readers and felt sure they would appreciate what he was trying to say. After almost two years of being rejected by more than 20 publishers, he decided to self-publish his book. Within the first few weeks of publication, *Immortals of Meluha* hit the bestseller charts. That's when the biggest publishers sat up. A bidding war ensued, and finally, Amish signed with Westland Books.

By this time, he had begun writing the sequel, *The Secret of the Nagas*. There were so many pre-orders for this book that Amish finally decided to quit his job and become a full-time author. He only left his job when he was earning as much from his royalties as his salary.

Success after Success

There was no stopping Amish now. Book after book spilled out of his pen. He wrote 11 books—both fiction and non-fiction, almost each one a bestseller. With his parents' advice never far from his mind, he remained open to any kind of opportunity. He played multiple roles. He worked as a diplomat, in the position of Minister for Culture and Education at the Indian High Commission in the UK, made television documentaries, wrote columns, and became a broadcaster. He has been declared the fastest-selling Indian author in the history of Indian publishing. He was included in the *Forbes* list of the 100 most influential people in India. He's won several international literary awards.

Amish Tripathi is nowhere near done. He is overflowing with ideas. He remains deeply inspired by ancient Indian culture and literature, and continues to promote it through his books. His advice to young people everywhere is: 'Follow your heart. But let your brain direct the journey.'

It's worked for him, as an adoring fan base awaits his next book.

23

YOGENDRA SINGH YADAV

The Young Hero

Young Yogendra waited eagerly for his father to come home on leave. Karan Singh Yadav, his father, was in the Indian Army with the 11 Kumaon Regiment. Yogendra loved to sit at his feet and listen for hours while his father regaled the family with stories of the army and its glorious deeds. It was the highlight of Yogendra's year. No wonder, then, that he went on to join the army and became a national hero.

Yogendra Singh was born on 10 May 1980 in Uttar Pradesh's Bulandshahr. Following his childhood dream,

Singh joined the armed forces when he was not quite 17. In 1996, he became a part of the Grenadiers, a section of the infantry known for its strength and skill in battle. As a junior commissioned officer (JCO), Yadav's rank was somewhere between that of a soldier and an officer.

A Bitter Battle

In 1999, tensions between India and its neighbour, Pakistan, were escalating. Pakistani troops, often disguised as Kashmiri militants, infiltrated into strategic positions on the Indian side of the LoC (line of control), as the border between the two countries is known. Incensed by the infiltration, the Indian Army and Air Force swung into action. A bitter battle ensued in the harsh and freezing terrain of Kargil, along the LoC, more than 16,000 feet above sea level.

As a grenadier, Yadav and his men found themselves in the thick of the battle. Tiger Hill, a steep mountain in the Dras region of Ladakh, was held by Pakistani troops. The Ghatak Commando Force of which Yadav was a part, along with 18 grenadiers, was tasked with capturing three bunkers on Tiger Hill. The bunkers were located at the top of a steep 1,000-foot cliff.

Leading the Way

Yadav eagerly volunteered to lead the assault and put up the ropes that would help him and his colleagues reach the summit. They believed they had the element of surprise on their side. But to their shock, when they were almost there, machine gun fire began to rain down on them. They had been spotted and the enemy had launched a fierce response.

Three members of Yadav's team, including their commander, were killed on the spot. Yadav himself was hit in the shoulder and groin. Ignoring the excruciating pain, he along with six of his team managed to evade more bullets. They reached the summit.

Now Yadav and his compatriots could not turn back, as the enemy had cut off their route. They had no idea how many soldiers were lying in wait for them at the summit. Indian troops, positioned a distance away, did however have a vantage view and began firing. The enemy responded with their firepower.

Yadav and his team decided to wait until they saw advancing Pakistani soldiers. Their patience paid off, and soon they spotted a small troop of enemy soldiers approaching stealthily. Yadav and his men opened fire. Five enemy soldiers were killed, while some escaped.

Never Giving up

The Pakistani army now began a serious assault. Using heavy machine guns and rocket-propelled grenades, they focused on the direction from which Yadav and company were shooting. All of Yadav's men were killed. He sustained severe bullet injuries. The seven bodies, Yadav one of them, lay piled on top of each other. Yadav lay still. The Pakistani soldiers thought he was dead, but they shot a few more bullets into him to be sure. It was a miracle that no bullet was fatal, but he now had 14 bullets in his body.

Yadav lay there, willing himself to stay alive. Eighteen Indian soldiers were trapped nearby. He was the only one still alive and knew where they were. He made it his mission to save them. Bleeding heavily and barely able to move, Yadav pulled out a grenade strapped to his belt. Struggling to move even a few inches, he removed the pin of the grenade and flung it with all his might at the approaching enemy soldiers. The grenade blew off a Pakistani soldier closest to Yadav. The body fell right on top of Yadav, who grabbed the dead soldier's rifle and began firing at the enemy, who mistook him for a corpse.

The Pakistani soldiers, who thought they had annihilated the Indian platoon, panicked. The sudden barrage of bullets from Yadav confused them and led them to think that Indian reinforcements had arrived. They retreated. Yadav crawled to his post, bloodied and injured, hoping to warn his colleagues. He saved their lives.

A Hero Returns

A group of deeply grateful Indian soldiers carried Yadav down Tiger Hill on their backs. He slipped in and out of consciousness, fighting for his life. He was taken to the base hospital in Srinagar and then to Delhi. There he lay in a coma for three days. When he woke up, his first question was how his battalion was doing.

He was told that thanks to his bravery and action, the Indian troops had conquered the heights without much resistance from the enemy. Yadav breathed a sigh of relief. He was only 19 years old, but he had acted with the bravery and presence of mind of a seasoned warrior. Yogendra Yadav will go down in history as one of the few brave soldiers to be awarded a Param Vir Chakra in his lifetime. He is also the youngest recipient of this honour.

Every year on 26 January, he proudly dons his uniform and leads the Republic Day parade, from an open jeep saluting the country he fought so hard for. He proved to the world that a hero knows no age.

24

MARY KOM

Woman with a Fighting Spirit

Ten-year-old Mary looked wistfully at the boys kicking a ball in the field just beyond the farm. She had no time to play. She had to help with washing the clothes, cleaning the dishes, looking after her younger siblings, and then lending a hand to her parents working on the farm.

'Come on, Mary,' her mother chided her. 'There's no time to daydream. You have a lot to finish.' Mary sighed and got on with her chores.

'One day...one day I will break free,' Mary vowed to herself silently. And she did. She went on to become a world-famous boxer, winning medals, awards and honours for her country at the highest levels, along the way emerging as a change-maker for women and girls everywhere. Not an easy task for a girl born into a poor family in a tiny village in the state of Manipur.

Life on a Farm

Mary's full name was Mangte Chungneijang Mary Kom, but she was simply known as Mary.

She was born in 1982 in a small hut. She didn't have a carefree childhood. Her parents were farm labourers and there wasn't much money. Mary's father was determined to give his children a proper education. So, besides all the work she did at home, she also had to manage her schoolwork.

It was in school that Mary discovered she enjoyed sports. She didn't do the things other girls did and would rather play volleyball with the boys. Her father noticed this but was helpless to support her in any way.

'Study well,' he would tell her. 'That is your only way out.'

Mary felt her future looked bleak unless she did something to help herself. She didn't want to work as a labourer on a farm all her life. When she was

15, she convinced her parents to let her leave home to go to a better school in Imphal, the capital city of Manipur. She would stay at the sports academy. This was where she would get the opportunity to train.

The Boxing Bug

It was here that Mary discovered boxing. She was a natural and found a coach who spotted her talent. The state coach, Narjit Singh, trained her, and she started winning fights—first at the school level and then at the state level.

All this while, her parents were clueless that she was getting serious about boxing. Her father was certain that once she had her fill of sports in general, she would marry, settle down, and have babies. After all, that was what women did.

In 1998, a young man from Manipur named Ngangom Dingko Singh won a gold medal in boxing at the Asian Games in Bangkok. When Mary heard about this, like many other Manipuri youngsters, she was inspired.

But Mary had a lot of hurdles to overcome. There was barely enough money to feed the family, so where would she get the money for her training? And the biggest hurdle of all was that she could never tell her parents about her secret ambition.

One day, her secret was out. Her name appeared in the local newspaper when she won the state championship in 2000. Her father was thunderstruck. Was that his Mary in the newspapers? At first, he was furious.

'Boxing is dangerous,' he said. 'It can damage your face, and then who will marry you?'

But when he calmed down, all he saw was his daughter's grit and determination. He relented and agreed to support her.

'To be a boxer and an athlete, you will need a good diet,' he told her worriedly. 'We can't afford that.'

'Don't worry,' Mary assured him, happy to have his support. 'I'll manage.'

So Many Problems

A good diet was the least of Mary's problems. Boxing was a male-dominated sport, and Mary was met with much scepticism at every stage. When she was selected to represent her country at the first Asian Women's Boxing Championships Meet in Bangkok, her passport was stolen on a train journey—and with it, the money she had collected for the trip.

Her parents, too proud to borrow money, sold the only cow they had. But family and friends came forward, and with their help, Mary was on her way. Her anxiety overwhelmed her, and she did not win. She came back humbled—but more determined than ever.

Supported by her parents, Mary began to take part in boxing events. With the first prize money she won, she bought a farm for her father so that they would never have to labour on someone else's farm again.

A Big Change

By now, Mary had given up her studies. Boxing was her world. She moved to Delhi for better training facilities. She could only speak Manipuri and the Kom language. Around this time, she met someone who became her lifelong support—Onler Kom, a man from her native Manipur.

Onler had been an aspiring athlete himself. In Mary, he saw the gumption and grit he so admired. He proposed to her. Mary also liked him a lot. The only condition she had was that he would never make her give up boxing after they were married. Onler willingly agreed. In 2005, Mary and Onler were married.

Mary was soon back in the ring, boxing harder than ever. She won many regional, national and international championships, but her heart was set on a gold medal at the Asian Games and the Olympics.

In 2007, another event occurred that changed Mary's life. She gave birth to twin boys. Everyone assumed that was the end of Mary's boxing career. Everyone except Onler and Mary. The twins were barely a year old when Mary left for a training camp that would be the selection ground for the fourth Asian Women's Championships.

Of Grit and Determination

Training became Mary's life for the next few years. She travelled to different places in India—sometimes with the twins. Her dream was to win at the 2012 London Olympics and the 2014 Asian Games.

Mary had fought in the 48 kg weight category. She was a small woman. But the lowest weight category at the Olympics was 51 kg. Mary was going to fight someone bigger and heavier than her. She worked hard and ate the right food to gain weight.

Mary made it through all the elimination rounds. In the Olympic semifinals, she fought desperately but lost. A part of her dream came true. She came home with a bronze medal.

But her dream of a major gold medal remained. She began preparing for the Asian Games in Bangkok. With the Olympics experience fresh in her mind, she worked on both her strength and her moves. This time, she made it to the finals.

The day of the final match arrived.

'MARY KOM! MARY KOM!' yelled the crowd as Mary entered the ring. Mary could not believe she actually had such a big following. Heartened, she took a deep breath. The referee blew the whistle, and the bout began. She had a strong opponent from Kazakhstan. Mary fought hard. She fought for her family. She fought for Manipur. And she fought for all the women athletes and boxers struggling to overcome prejudice.

SHE WON! The gold was hers. She had a lump in her throat as she saw the Indian flag being hoisted, and the crowd erupted in cheers.

Mary Kom not only made her dream come true but also paved the way for other female athletes who had a dream. She went on to win many more medals, awards and accolades. The Olympic bronze in 2012, the first Indian female boxer to win gold at the 2014 Asian Games, the Padma Vibhushan, the Padma Bhushan, the Padma Shri, the Rajiv Gandhi Khel Ratna Award, and the Arjuna Award are just some of the honours that came her way.

She was now known as Magnificent Mary. She showed the world what a true fighting spirit meant.

25

Neeraj Chopra

The Man with the Magic Throw

'Drink it up,' said his grandmother lovingly, pulling her grandson onto her lap. She watched affectionately as the young boy drank a large glass of thick milk and followed it with another, full of cream and sugar. This was Neeraj's daily ritual with his *dadi* after school. Little did she know that her cute, plump grandson would one day become a lean, muscular javelin star and India's pride and joy.

A Chance Discovery

Neeraj Chopra was born in 1997 in a tiny village called Khandra in Panipat district of Haryana. His large family of 19 included uncles, aunts, cousins and grandparents. It was a simple farming family. Like so many boys his age, Neeraj was quite naughty. He would tie the tails of two cows together and then hide to watch the fun. And, like it was for so many boys in India, the only game he knew was cricket. He had never even heard of a javelin.

One day, one of his three uncles decided it was time to do something about Neeraj.

'He's getting too plump,' his uncles declared. 'All that milk and cream is not good for him.' There was a brief family conference. Neeraj was to be enrolled at the village gym to get him in shape. Neeraj cheerfully accepted, as he was fed up with being teased at school. But as luck would have it, the gym shut down.

'He needs a personal trainer,' the family decided. Neeraj was whisked off to the larger city of Panipat, where there were more facilities than in the small village of Khandra. One day, after his workout, Neeraj found himself at the Shivaji Stadium of Panipat. Some youngsters were practising javelin throwing.

Neeraj watched in fascination as a strange, spear-like object flew gracefully through the air. He badly wanted to try it out. He made friends with Jaiveer Choudhary, a local javelin thrower.

'Want to try?' Jaiveer asked him one day, seeing how keen Neeraj was. Neeraj nodded eagerly. Imitating Jaiveer, he ran and threw the javelin with all his might. The javelin flew far and high—an amazing throw for someone who had never held a javelin in his life. Jaiveer was impressed. He decided to take Neeraj under his wing.

A New Life

Life changed for Neeraj. He had found his passion. He began to train seriously. He took part in local junior athletic meets and began to win. He now needed a good javelin. Seeing his progress, his father and uncles put money together and bought him his first javelin. Neeraj cleaned it and looked after it, as it was his most precious belonging.

He became so good at throwing the javelin that his family decided he needed proper coaching. He moved to Panchkula, where he began training under a local coach, Naseem Ahmed. Neeraj was a very conscientious lad. To get rid of his baby fat, he was made to run cross-country along with middle- and long-distance runners. He didn't complain because he knew it would improve his run-up while throwing the javelin. His family didn't have enough money for advanced coaching, but he learnt by watching videos of international javelin champions. He carefully observed the angle at which they held the javelin, the cross-steps they took before the throw, the release, and the follow-through. Slowly he got better and better. He won the bronze medal at a district championship.

Success after Success

Neeraj was now truly on his way. He won the gold medal at the National Junior Athletics Championships. With a throw of over 68 metres, he set a new national record. By then, there was no doubt in anyone's mind that Neeraj was made for bigger things. But access to training and coaching at the highest level was still difficult. That's when fate—and a talent scout—intervened.

One day, during the National Junior Athletics Championships in Lucknow, a sports talent scout from JSW Sports, an organization that helped athletes with their training, spotted Neeraj. Impressed by his abilities and grit, he was drafted into JSW Sports. Suddenly the world opened up for Neeraj. He now had access to the best equipment, international coaches, and training.

Neeraj's entire focus was now on his sport. So, imagine his surprise when a most unexpected job offer came his way. Impressed by his performance, the Indian Army offered him a direct appointment as a junior commissioned officer in the Rajputana Rifles regiment—something that was rare. Of course, Neeraj was not expected to actually report to duty every day. This job was meant more to offer him security so that he could focus on training.

And he did. Neeraj focused on his sport with complete dedication. Nothing else mattered to him. He began competing at international level, making his mark in the process—a silver medal at the Youth Olympic Games qualification, a gold at the Asian Games, a world record in the junior category with a stunning throw of over 81 metres.

But even as his medal tally and successes continued to grow, Neeraj had his sights set on the highest of them all—a gold medal at the Olympics. But fate intervened once again, and he suffered a terrible elbow injury. It brought his training to a grinding halt. Many worried that this was the end of his career, because how was a javelin thrower supposed to function with an impaired elbow?

But Neeraj was unfazed. He underwent critical surgery. He could not throw a javelin for 16 long months, but he threw himself into rehabilitation with his customary determination. Then came the pandemic, and his training had to take a back seat. Through it all, Neeraj remained focused on his single goal—the 2021 Tokyo Olympics.

Preparing for the Tokyo Olympics was a Herculean task—but not one that Neeraj shied away from. On the contrary, it gave him a burst of energy. Working closely with his German coach, Klaus Bartonietz, a biomechanics expert, he worked tirelessly on his technique even as he built his speed and strength. To prepare for the Olympics, he went to Uppsala in Sweden, where the facilities were better.

The Biggest of Them All

Finally, after months of intense training, the big day arrived. Neeraj was ready, but he was also anxious. His main competitor, the German athlete Johannes Vetter, had thrown at a distance of 90 metres—much more than Neeraj's best. Surpassing this mark would be tough. But Neeraj was primed and ready. He had aced the qualifiers with a throw that would have won him gold anyway, as he realized later.

It was a big moment and the eyes of over a billion Indians were on him. The entire village of Khandra was glued to their TV sets, praying to various gods, keeping their fingers crossed and their lucky talismans ready.

Neeraj was calm. He had only one thing on his mind—the gold medal. Every instruction, every bit of training, every last tip his coach had given him was clear in his mind.

He took a deep breath and ran. With every stride, he picked up pace. He stretched out his elbows until the angle was just right. And then, his wrist at just the right angle, he released the javelin. It shot out of his hands as if a bullet was being shot from a gun. The javelin sailed high and far. It crossed the 87-metre mark, landing sharply on the ground at 87.58 metres.

The stadium and the country held their collective breath as Johannes Vetter, his chief rival, came running in. Ninety metres had become his new normal. But the pressure got to him and his javelin landed at 82.52 metres. The next closest throw, by the Czech athlete Jakub Vadlejch, fell far below Neeraj's at 86.67 metres, winning him the silver.

The stadium rose in applause. Neeraj knew in his heart the gold was his. And then it was announced. Khandra, Panipat and Panchkula exploded with joy.

Millions of Indians cheered as the Indian flag was raised, and Neeraj bowed his head to accept his gold medal.

At just 24 years of age, Neeraj Chopra was a hero to millions. When he came back to India, the entire country was waiting to welcome him. Over the next few months, he was feted and felicitated, as lucrative advertising contracts poured in, changing his life completely. But Neeraj did not change. He remained the same humble, hardworking boy he always had been. He was happy with his success, but now he had a new goal. He wanted to cross the 90-metre mark with his throw.

It was now time for the 2024 Olympics. Neeraj packed his bags and headed to Paris, full of determination. His only goal was to breach the 90-metre mark. Neeraj threw with everything he had. His first few throws fell short. The gold went to Arshad Nadeem—a good friend of Neeraj's—who, with a throw of 92.97 metres, achieved a new Olympic record. Neeraj finally landed his career's second best at 89.49 metres, winning the silver medal.

Neeraj may not have won gold, but he continues to be determined to achieve his goal. He showed the world one thing—that a true athlete always strives for excellence. His journey continues.